The Public Manager Case Book

The Public Manager Case Book

Making Decisions in a Complex World

Edited by

Terrel L. Rhodes
Portland State University

SAGE Publications
International Educational and Professional Publisher
Thousand Oaks ▪ London ▪ New Delhi

For information:

Sage Publications, Inc.
2455 Teller Road
Thousand Oaks, California 91320
E-mail: order@sagepub.com

Sage Publications Ltd.
6 Bonhill Street
London EC2A 4PU
United Kingdom

Sage Publications India Pvt. Ltd.
M-32 Market
Greater Kailash I
New Delhi 110 048 India

Printed in the United States of America

Library of Congress Cataloging-in-Publication Data (to come)

The public manager case book: Making decisions in a complex world / editor, Terrel L. Rhodes.
 p. cm.
Includes bibliographical references and index.
 ISBN 0-7619-2327-6 (p)
 1. Public administration—Case studies. 2. Public administration—United States. I. Rhodes, Terrel L., 1949-
JF1351 .P836 2003
 352.3'3—dc21   2002002729

02 03 04 05 10 9 8 7 6 5 4 3 2 1

Acquiring Editor:	Marquita Flemming
Editorial Assistant:	MaryAnn Vail
Production Editor:	Diane S. Foster
Copy Editor:	Jon Preimesberger
Typesetter:	C&M Digitals (P), Ltd., Chennai, India
Proofer:	Scott Oney
Indexer:	Molly Hall
Cover Designer:	Michelle Lee

Contents

Introduction

Public administration and public policy programs as academic disciplines have struggled since their inception with the need to provide theoretical and conceptual grounding for their respective fields and the need to link theory with practice. Incorporating theory and research from many other disciplines, the study of public organizations and policies has typically followed the traditional pattern of organizing and presenting material through course work. Students have studied discrete courses in human resources and personnel, budget and finance issues and processes, organizational behavior and development, administrative decision making, program evaluation and policy analysis, ethics, and strategic planning. Often, students completed their course of study with a capstone seminar in problem solving, or some type of thesis project designed to integrate the previous course work.

Rarely have students been presented with an opportunity to examine the diverse theories and information learned in the discrete courses of the curriculum through the application of the theories and knowledge in the context of resolving actual problems or issues confronted by practicing administrators in the public arena. Case analysis provides a vehicle for students to integrate and apply their knowledge to situations that confront practicing managers in their day-to-day positions.

Earlier casebooks in public administration and public policy have tended to focus on national or even international situations or policies with which the general population would have some familiarity. The reality of public administration, though, is that most public managers find themselves in local and state-level positions. These managers spend their time dealing with the less exciting issues that are of immediate importance to those involved. Managers who planned to spend their careers in a specific area of the public sector (e.g., human resources management) soon discover that on the job they are asked to make decisions requiring the integration of personnel theory and knowledge with budget, ethics, organizational dynamics, and many other areas from their administrative training.

The current text presents eight cases that represent actual, real-world situations that required public managers to act. Each case requires the managers to draw from a variety of discrete public administration or policy knowledge areas to develop alternative recommendations, decisions, or actions to try to resolve a specific situation. In some instances the names and places have been changed, but each case is an actual situation that public managers confronted and had to resolve. A variety of information and resources to assist in addressing each case is provided for the student and for the instructor. A variety of pedagogical strategies can also be used to engage students and to achieve analysis of the case materials.

The Cases

Case 1, *Balancing the Budget in Gaston County, North Carolina*, highlights the complex balancing process between budget construction and approval. The competing demands to limit public expenditures versus generation of new revenue, or tax increases, to meet budget demands is central to this case. The role of the public administrator and the values that underlie the budget recommendations often conflict with the elected officials' values and priorities. Individual ethics and personality further generate a challenging set of events for public officials.

Case 2, *Emergency Management at the Millennium: The Role of Information Systems*, focuses on the decision to upgrade the emergency information system used by the police department. A central role for government has traditionally been the provision of police and fire protection and the response to emergency situations. Technology has allowed emergency response agencies to respond much more rapidly than in the past. As a result, citizens expect that a top priority of local government is to provide a quick response time to their emergency calls. The fear that computer-driven technology would not be able to handle emergency responses as a result of the Y2K "computer bug" as the new millennium arrived, prompted great concern and action to avoid any interruption in emergency service. Interdepartmental conflicts, the role of long-term employees as keepers of institutional memory, and internal versus external consultant recommendations and analysis converge under a critical time-sensitive decision-making process as computer clocks tick toward the year 2000.

Case 3, *The Quest to Continue: Healthy Communities, Inc.*, introduces the role of nonprofit organizations in the delivery of services and the problems that confront these nongovernmental organizations. Without the numerous nonprofit organizations across the United States and the world, many of the services citizens receive would never be available. The costs of public services would be substantially higher if local and state governments had to provide all of the services that people receive from nonprofit agencies. Public governmental service providers typically have statutory existence that is not shared by nonprofit groups. Nonprofits rely on varied funding streams to exist, along with a mixture of citizen volunteers and paid employees. Nonprofits confront issues similar to governmental agencies in meeting needs of the community, but they also must contend with a more volatile and uncertain environment to sustain their very existence.

Case 4, *Ending Welfare as We Know It? Cabarrus County Implements Welfare Reform*, traces state and local efforts to reform welfare. The movement to change welfare programs from entitlement programs to programs designed to transition people into employment, prompted many different approaches to accomplishing the objective. Political ideologies, partisan politics, and professional practice played out at national, state, and local levels. Local elected officials, state officials, and local public administrators jockeyed over potentially conflicting approaches. Rank-and-file administrative personnel demonstrated both effective performance and resistance to changes in policy and organization. The problems of limited control exercised by public managers and multilayered decision making permeate the process.

Case 5, *Evolving Objectives: The Statewide Evaluation and Planning Services Program*, examines nursing home policy development through the presentation of an evaluation of the existing program. Program evaluation is a vehicle for examination of the impact of various strategies for providing nursing home care. The role of federal and state intergovernmental relations in the adoption of policies with overlapping jurisdiction and consequences, administrative discretion and limits of control, and formal and informal bureaucratic structures affected the delivery of services for individuals in need of nursing home care. The role of public administrators, the need to meet statutory requirements, and the needs of the public collide in interesting ways as local jurisdictions attempt to provide services.

Case 6, *Teaching What They Practice*, illustrates critical ethical dilemmas faced in the delivery of medical services when span of control and ability to influence decision making and oversight are constrained. Leadership, or lack of it, coupled with a teaching environment creates serious risk management issues for an individual placed in a position with conflicting pressures. Not only human resources management issues, but serious violations of law and regulations create dilemmas for individuals who respond in very different ways to the problematic practices.

Case 7, *The Edifice Complex: A New Coliseum for Charlotte?*, focuses on a private and public partnership surrounding the effort to construct a new sports stadium. The case illustrates an important dimension of many local economies—the sports as entertainment sector—and the dilemmas presented by the cooperation of government and private enterprises. The interplay among public administrators, public-elected officials, corporate owners, and the general citizenry and voters is sharply illustrated through the sequence of events and actions that revolved around a proposal to construct a new stadium for a professional basketball team. Students not only examine the financial aspects of the decision, but also the efforts to build consensus among community leaders and public officials, and the importance of media, public perceptions, and the role of democratic processes in making decisions about public action and investment.

Case 8, *Smart Cards for Paperless Transactions: Facilitation of e-Government or Threat to Security?*, provides an example of leadership in the application of e-government to address a wide variety of citizen and government needs. The movement within the public arena to become more efficient elicits the examination of e-government solutions for the provision of government services and transactions. Issues of the span of services, the process for determining which services to provide in what manner creates strong contention among decision-makers. At the same time, issues of rights of individuals and responsibilities of public agencies emerge forcefully in the decision-making process to determine the best way to proceed. Privacy versus efficiency, individual rights versus governmental authority, and the appropriate use of technology in the service of democratic society collide through an agenda designed to establish national leadership. This final case also demonstrates the globalization of issues that confront public officials around the world. Further, the possibility or desire to pursue technology as a means available to less developed areas to level the economic playing field in the provision of services to its people, does not always come without substantial costs.

To the Student

Students, you will find a variety of situations included in the cases. It is not likely that any one of you would ever encounter all of these situations in your professional career. However, it is likely that you will encounter situations that will involve similar sets of competing demands, decision and policy makers sitting in different levels of government, and conflicting values and objectives. Situations that you will have to resolve, or at least propose some potential solutions for resolving, are usually not simple or easy.

At the conclusion of this introduction is a table that summarizes some of the key theoretical and conceptual issues in each of the cases. The table is a shorthand guide to key issues that you may have initial interest in examining. Alternatively, the table may serve as a guide to aspects of the particular case that you may wish to focus your attention on as you read each situation.

For some cases, you will want more information. In other cases, you will feel overwhelmed by the information provided. One of the learning objectives for case analysis is to experience the need to examine critically what information is actually necessary for making a decision or recommending a course of action, and which information may not be essential. You may find that you can locate and focus new information on the case, or you may find that, quite frankly, the information that you would really like to have to make a decision is not available. You may discover that the absolutely best recommendation you devise, bolstered by the best evidence there is, will be ignored by other, perhaps more influential decision makers. Or, you may find that long efforts to ground your recommendations in logical, well-supported data and best practice, is overcome by public perception or political expediency, resulting in an outcome that you find to be less desirable.

Frustration is a common sentiment that you will likely experience while engaged in case analyses. Appreciation for both the limitations of you as an individual administrator, and the reality that virtually all

Major Topics in Case Studies

Topics	Case 1 Gaston County	Case 2 Emergency Management	Case 3 Healthy Communities	Case 4 Welfare to Work	Case 5 STEPS Health	Case 6 Teaching Practice	Case 7 Edifice Complex	Case 8 e-Government Smart Cards
Accountability	X	X	X		X		X	X
Managerial Discretion and Ethics	X	X			X	X		X
Formal/Informal Structures of Bureaucracy					X	X		X
Decision Making Under Uncertainty		X	X		X			
Collaboration and Cooperation		X	X		X			
Leadership Style	X	X	X			X	X	X
Human Resources	X		X		X			
Program Design and Change		X	X	X	X			
Limits of Control		X		X	X	X	X	
Policy Analysis and Program Evaluation		X		X	X		X	X
Budget and Finance	X		X				X	
Citizen Rights and Liberties	X		X				X	X
Intergovernmental Relations		X		X	X			
Politics	X	X	X	X			X	X
Public/Private Partnerships	X						X	
Human Services	X		X	X	X			
Service Delivery		X	X	X	X	X		X
Communication		X	X		X	X	X	X

public decisions will at some point never be individual decisions is a powerful moment of awareness for public servants. This realization might be termed humility. It is the realization that as a public administrator, you are only one of many people who are involved in formulating, defining, constructing, implementing, and analyzing policies, procedures, and service delivery. Your role as an administrator requires you to be as well prepared as possible as a professional, to be thorough and fair in your presentation of information, and to advocate for decisions and actions that honor the public good. In the course of day-to-day life, the actual experience is typically not as clear, orderly, or noble; however, somewhat surprisingly, theory and practice do complement each other most of the time.

The cases that follow will ask you to draw on the knowledge and skills gained in the formal courses, readings, and research in which you have been engaged. For some of you, the on-the-job experience you have will inform you. In most of the cases, there is not one correct answer. Outcomes depend very heavily on the individuals involved, the information that is available, and the perceptions and circumstances prevailing at the time a decision or recommendation is required. Part of the learning is examining why one conclusion was reached rather than another.

1

Balancing the Budget in Gaston County, North Carolina

David F. Thompson and Gary R. Rassel

❖ BACKGROUND

Gaston County, population 190,365, is located in the southwest central part of North Carolina in the metropolitan area of Charlotte. Historically the predominant industry in the county was textiles. Agriculture was also important. In recent years the textile industry declined and county leaders attempted to diversify the local economy. Although the metropolitan region grew substantially in the decade between 1990 and 2000, Gaston County's population growth and its economy lagged behind that of the region. County government employed approximately 1,200 people. In many ways, the county was highly urbanized as it had 15 incorporated towns and cities, more than all but two of North Carolina's 100 counties. The city of Gastonia was the largest city in the county with a population of 66,300. However, a substantial proportion of the county population lived in rural areas outside of any municipality.

The county was governed by a seven-member elected board of commissioners who appointed a county manager responsible for administration. The manager served at the pleasure of the commission. In addition to the manager, top administrative officials included a deputy manager and an assistant manager. The chair of the board of commissioners during the fiscal year 2002 budget crisis was Heath Jenkins, who became chair after two years into his first term with the support of three newly elected commissioners. Although all members of the board were Republicans, votes of 4 to 3 were common with the chair usually voting with the majority.

State law specified that one of the duties of the county manager was to develop and present annually a balanced budget to the county commissioners. The law also required the county commissioners to adopt a balanced budget by July 1 of each year. State law required local governments to operate on a fiscal year beginning July 1 and ending June 30 of the following calendar year. During the fiscal year 2000–2001, when the budget for the next year was developed, the county's property tax rate was 82.5 cents per $100 of assessed value, the highest in the region. At that rate, an owner of a $100,000 home would pay $825 in county property taxes. Although this appeared low by comparison with local tax rates in other parts of the nation, rates in the six North Carolina counties surrounding Gaston ranged from a low of 47 cents per $100 of assessed value to a high of 73 cents per $100.

During the second week of January 2001, the county commissioners convened at a retreat to preview the needs and policies for the upcoming budget. The goal that the board members agreed to pursue was a budget with no tax increase. They also planned to look at the effectiveness of all county departments and the appropriateness of their funding levels. The county budget for the fiscal year 2000–2001 was $171,287,226. At the time of the retreat, County Manager Phil Hinely projected a budget shortfall of $15.6 million for the 2001–2002 fiscal year budget. He projected this shortfall by comparing the anticipated revenues for the upcoming fiscal year with the current fiscal year (2000–2001) expenditures. Thus, the shortfall did not take into account any potential increases in county expenditures for the new fiscal year.

Chairman Jenkins stated that he planned "to get the commissioners thinking well before crunch time in the spring," and he asked Hinely "what the board could do now to ease money troubles." Hinely stated that the county was looking at parts of the budget it could change and that the major expenditures were related to personnel costs. Hinely proposed not filling positions for the rest of the current fiscal year but noted that this simply carried the funding problem forward to the next year's budget.

The county's annual financial audit was also presented at the commissioners' retreat meeting. The external auditor reported that the "fund balance has dropped in all categories over the last three years." In previous years the commissioners had avoided tax hikes by tapping the fund balances of the county to enable them to enact a balanced budget. Thus, they appropriated fund balance to help cover operational expenses during the years leading up to the current one.

Also during January 2001, state government analysts predicted that North Carolina could face a budget shortfall of at least $486 million. This anticipated shortfall was even greater than the projection made in the fall of 2000 when state analysts had estimated that revenues would fall $350 million short of balancing the state budget. State government budget problems affected counties in North Carolina because the state government returned a substantial portion of revenue to the counties. With the state government facing a revenue shortfall, state officials announced plans to withhold local government reimbursements.

The state's fiscal situation stemmed from both revenue and expenditure problems. These included tax collections that were already $149 million short of the projections for the first five months of the fiscal year, two unexpected judgments against the state for $59 million in taxes paid by two major corporations, Medicaid program costs that were $108 million over budget, and individual tax refunds totaling $122 million that had been deferred to the current year. In addition, the state had reduced corporate business taxes and granted other tax breaks in previous years. Continuing state expenses to help parts of North Carolina recover from major flooding caused by Hurricane Floyd in the fall of 1999 also took a toll. Thus, at the beginning of Gaston County's budget deliberations, the state of North Carolina was beginning to address its own budget crisis, which then would impact Gaston County negatively. The challenge to the Gaston County commissioners was to balance the budget in the face of reduced revenues while holding true to the majority of the board members' desire to avoid raising taxes.

❖ THE BUDGET

The budget development cycle for the Gaston County commissioners began in January 2001 with an estimated shortfall of $16 million for a budget of approximately $171,300,000 and would end with the adoption of a balanced budget in June 2001.

During the summer of 2000, before work on the 2001–2002 fiscal year budget began, the county had implemented a plan to avoid filling 30 vacant positions. County budget staff had originally estimated that this action would enable the county to save $1.4 million. However, staff later found that the actual savings were just $642,000. The commissioners then implemented a 30-day hiring delay for all new employees in an attempt to capture the full $1.4 million in savings as they began preparations for developing a budget for the next fiscal year.

Before going into the January budget retreat, the chairman of the board proposed publicly through the local newspaper that the county institute a hiring freeze with no time limit to apply to all county departments. Chairman Jenkins stated, "Those are jobs that are already vacant. I'm not talking about laying anyone off or firing anyone."

In reporting on this suggested freeze, the local media mentioned a major problem created during the previous fiscal year. The county commissioners had appropriated $16 million from the county's fund balances for the 2000–2001 fiscal year operating budget. The Budget Department recommended that the board not use the savings account this year as a strategy to balance the upcoming budget. Thus, because the operating deficit was not addressed the previous year through identifying revenues, the board was faced with having to make up the current year's deficit as well as dealing with the growth of expenditures that would hit the county for the next fiscal year.

After commissioners approved the hiring freeze, they were immediately deluged with requests for exemptions from county department heads. The human resources director stated that the majority of the 61 vacant positions at that time were in areas that the commissioners might consider vital to public safety. This was important because the commissioners had stated that they would consider exemptions to this freeze for public health and safety services. The human resources director subtracted positions that were categorized as having public safety implications. These positions included protective social workers, jailers, paramedics, 911 (emergency call) dispatchers, animal control officers, health department nurses, and environmental health inspectors. He also pointed out that many of the 61 positions were funded by federal and state grants that would be lost if the positions were eliminated. With these positions subtracted, the estimated savings amounted to only $200,000. The commissioners in subsequent meetings exempted many of the vacant positions from the freeze after reviewing the requests of the different agencies and, thus, the estimated savings were minimal.

Before the board's budget retreat, commissioners began reviewing different cost-saving ideas such as reducing the county's motor fleet. This review and that of other operations failed to generate any substantial savings. "We need to do all of these things, but I don't see any way out of a tax increase this year," said Commissioner Joe Carpenter. Commissioner Carpenter maintained this position throughout budget deliberations.

During the annual retreat, the budget and revenue shortfall dominated the board's discussions. The county manager told the commissioners that most of the budget was spent on state and federally mandated programs. He informed them that they controlled only about $50 million out of the current budget of approximately $170 million. "We have about $50 million to find $16 million," said Commissioner Tom Keigher. The commissioners went on to discuss items that could be cut in amounts as large as $3.7 million for public school teacher supplements to items as small as the Farm Service Agency's annual appropriation of $650. The board also discussed selling different assets for one-time windfalls. The most controversial proposed asset sale was to sell the county hospital, Gaston Memorial Hospital.

Gaston County leased Gaston Memorial Hospital to CaroMont Health, a private company that operated it. Commissioner Keigher stated that he did not believe the county should be the hospital's landlord. "I believe that this county, or any government should not be in the business of anything but government," he said. "Selling the hospital property could bring in between $250 million and $400 million," County Manager Phil Hinely said. This discussion created a lively debate among the commissioners and in the community. The original decision to lease Gaston Memorial Hospital to a private corporation had been controversial. The level of control that the board was to have over the hospital and its role in the provision of health care to the community were in dispute and debated.

Another controversial issue discussed during the commissioners' budget retreat was a proposal to consolidate the Gaston County Police Department with other law enforcement entities in the county. Gaston County was one of two counties in North Carolina with separate police and sheriff's departments. The county police provided law enforcement in the unincorporated areas whereas the sheriff provided several other traditional services, such as maintaining the jail and delivering subpoenas. The county police also provided law enforcement to some of the smaller towns in the county under contract. The deputy county manager had been serving as the director of public safety, a position that included responsibility for the county police.

The commissioners discussed merging the county police with the Sheriff's Department or combining the county police with the Gastonia Police Department to save money. The Gaston County Police Department employed 137 sworn officers and 86 nonsworn employees, while the Sheriff's Department employed a total of 187 sworn and nonsworn employees. The Gastonia Police Department had 260 employees. Thus, several commissioners thought merging functions and eliminating overlap could result in considerable savings. This issue would prove to be one of the more controversial ones driven by the budget shortfall. The deputy county manager had voiced his opposition to the merger of the county police with the Gastonia Police Department or the Sheriff's Department.

The commissioners ended their retreat without any firm ideas about what they needed to do to balance the budget for the upcoming year. However, they had raised several issues that further complicated their budget deliberations. Two of these issues, the sale of the hospital and the merger of the county police with other entities, dominated many of their discussions from January until budget adoption in June.

From Bad to Worse

In February, the state budget analysts increased the estimates of the state's revenue shortfall from the earlier $496 million figure to a shortage in the range of $605 to $791 million. Governor Mike Easley invoked emergency powers under the state constitution and announced a massive $558 million in state budget adjustments. These included taking money from the state's rainy day fund, holding back money owed to cities and counties, and dipping into state employees' pension funds. A major impact on cities and counties was the withholding of $95 million in reimbursements for the defunct "inventory tax." The state had eliminated this tax on retail store and company inventories ten years earlier. Because the local governments had collected and received that tax, the state had "held them harmless" and provided a reimbursement for lost revenue. The revenue loss for the 2001–2002 fiscal year to Gaston County from the governor's withholding of these reimbursements amounted to as much as $2 million.

This move by state government compounded the problems faced by Gaston County. It was virtually impossible for the state to consider increasing revenue options for local governments because that was perceived by many state officials as reducing the revenue options for state government. Gaston County, nevertheless, decided to lobby for the authority to generate more revenue by increasing the local option sales tax. Other cities and counties did the same and received the same response of little support from the North Carolina General Assembly because of the state worries about its own revenue shortfall and overall concerns about tax increases that were beginning to appear inevitable.

In February 2001, Gaston County increased the estimate of its shortfall to a range of $16 to $18 million. This was reported to the media. The commissioners voted to postpone most of the county's building and renovation projects in an effort to reduce expenditures.

During the first week in March, county commissioners attended a legislative conference in Washington, DC. While talking together in a hotel lobby, Chairman Jenkins and Vice Chairman Donnie Loftis asked County Manager Hinely to resign. Returning to Gaston County, Hinely met in a closed session with the commissioners. After he came out of this session, he announced his resignation. At the commission's next regular meeting the commissioners voted 4 to 2 to accept his resignation with one commissioner not present because of illness. At this meeting and for weeks afterward, the community showed widespread support for Hinely. Citizen statements to the media clearly revealed that they thought Hinely was the scapegoat for the financial problems the county was facing, because he had warned the commissioners during the previous year's budget sessions that the fund balances should not be raided to fund the operating budget. The commissioners authorized a severance package for Hinely that approached $250,000 plus health insurance for life. They were criticized intensely for firing the person who many citizens perceived had the most expertise about the county's finances, and for compounding the county's financial problems with the payment of the $250,000.

After Hinely's resignation, Assistant County Manager Phil Ponder was appointed to be interim county manager, bypassing the deputy county manager who had more experience and seniority. At that time, a new commissioner was sworn into office to replace a commissioner who had resigned because of health problems. Both of these actions took place during a critical period of the budget's preparation.

Before receiving the manager's budget, the county commissioners had managed to reduce the shortfall by almost $2.5 million by eliminating approximately 30 vacant jobs in the Department of Social Services and reducing expenditures for public works projects. However, the county's economy suffered another blow in the spring as more than 1,000 workers in the region were laid off from April to June.

Before presenting his budget to the commissioners on May 31, Interim Manager Ponder implied that it would be a dismal budget. "Now is the time to give them something that I feel will address the needs of the county in terms of where we're at right now," Ponder said. "I think it's my job to give them something, as ugly as it may be and as unpopular as it may be." By the time the interim manager's budget was presented, the estimate of the shortfall had grown to $20.2 million. This shortfall was the difference between what county government agencies and departments had requested for the next year and the revenues that county staff estimated would be available. This estimate took into account the withholding of the state's inventory tax reimbursements, increases in Medicaid costs, and growing debt service payments for major construction initiatives of previous years.

Recommended Budget Presented to Commissioners

Interim Manager Ponder's recommended budget for fiscal year 2001–2002 of $170,937,215 amounted to a decrease of $605,924 from the projected expenditures for fiscal year 2000–2001. The proposed budget contained large cuts in expenditures along with a 9-cent increase in the property tax rate. The proposed budget would raise taxes from 82.5 cents per $100 of assessed property valuation to 91.5 cents. The annual county tax bill for the owner of a $100,000 home would rise by $90 from $825 to $915. Some of the highlights of the county budget were a spending cut of approximately $7 million from building projects, a decrease of $2.9 million from operating costs mainly by eliminating vacant positions, an elimination of a cost-of-living pay increase in the amount of $650,000, and no increase in funding to Gaston County schools, Gaston Community College, or nonprofit agencies. Ponder even recommended eliminating his previous position of assistant county manager.

The board members were unanimous in stating that they did not believe that a tax increase of 9 cents would be acceptable. "I don't think the majority of this board is prepared to raise taxes by 9 cents," said Commission Chairman Jenkins. "Nobody's going to want a 9-cent tax increase," Commissioner Pearl Floyd said. "How are retired citizens going to pay that? They're living on a fixed income. Fuel prices have gone up. Utility prices have gone up." Commissioner Floyd Wright, who campaigned on a "no tax increase" pledge, stated that he preferred layoffs to a tax increase if it came to that. "I don't want a 9-cent tax increase. I don't think the wealthiest person in the county wants a 9-cent tax increase," said Commissioner Keigher. The only member of the board who stated his support for a 9-cent tax increase was Commissioner Carpenter. He stated that this would help remove some of the burden that the county would face in the budget following the one being currently debated.

The media immediately began quoting county employees concerned about the proposed budget, but at the same time the media found support for Ponder as the interim manager. The public's concern was focused on service levels, possible job layoffs, and the retention of remaining employees.

Across-the-Board Cuts Proposed

During the middle of June, the county commissioners focused on a new plan to avoid a tax increase. They restored capital projects to the budget while at the same time calling for an 8.7% cut across all of county government. "That's the only thing I'm going to vote for," Commissioner Wright said of the plan. Interim Manager Ponder reminded the Board that at their request he had previously shown the board the impact of a 7.5% reduction across the board, the elimination of capital projects, and no tax increase. Commissioner Keigher argued against the equal percentage cuts proposal and reaffirmed that he felt each department was different and should be considered differently. At the end of the session, Ponder stated that he was not sure of what the board had requested. "I will do whatever this board asks me to do, but I'm a little unclear as to what you want me to bring you that I haven't already brought to you," he said. Chairman Jenkins said the overall goal was to maintain a no-tax-increase budget with an across-the-board spending cut. The board could then raise to previous budget levels select items that it felt should not be cut.

The board held a public hearing on the budget two days after discussing the 8.7% across-the-board cut and heard from numerous citizens that they would rather have a tax rate increase than the proposed reductions. The most vocal group was composed of school supporters.

The superintendent of schools informed the commissioners that he would prefer not to fire classroom teachers, and that students would feel the effects of budget reductions if schools had to trim programs such as athletics, art, and music. In follow-up media coverage, board members began to second-guess what their peers' positions would be. Chairman Jenkins expected the board to raise taxes but not as much as the 9-cent increase that Interim Manager Ponder recommended. Commissioner Wright backed the 8.7% cut and felt that commissioners Price and Loftis would back that reduction. The newest member of the board, Commissioner Floyd, expected the commissioners to raise taxes but not as much as 9 cents and did not support the 8.7% cut. Commissioner Keigher stated that he thought that Jenkins, Wright, Price, and Loftis had already planned to vote for the 8.7% cut and stated they were just trying to appear sympathetic.

Department heads began to discuss publicly how their budgets would look with this type of reduction and also reacted negatively to statements from commissioners that some departments, such as schools and public safety agencies, would be spared. One example given was that the health department budget would have to be slashed by 48%, which would require eliminating all functions and staff that were not state-mandated.

The Gaston County Board of Education began discussing the possibility of legal action if the commissioners reduced the school's budget by 8.7%. This cut would amount to a reduction in their current budget of almost $2.5 million. Board of education members stated that the best resolution would be to receive the same funding that they received during the current budget year.

During the next-to-last week of budget deliberations, the county commission in a work session voted 4 to 3 to cut allocations to public safety and education by the same percentage but did not specify the percentage. This was on a Thursday night. On the preceding Monday the same four commissioners had voted on a 5% cut to Gaston County Police, Sheriff's Department, and Gaston Emergency Medical Services. The reason given for lowering the recommended cuts from 8.7% to 5% was that the commissioners felt the 8.7% reduction would prove to be too severe for these departments. However, a 5% reduction would still eliminate 13 positions in the Gaston County Police Department, 37 jailers from the Sheriff's Department, and six paramedics from Emergency Medical Services. During the board's meeting, an audience composed mainly of school supporters expressed their negative opinions on treating schools in the same manner as public safety when cuts were being considered. The county commissioners proposed reducing the next year's appropriation to the school system by $880,000, which would have given them less than the current year's appropriation. After three hours of reviewing the budget again, the commissioners were shocked to discover that to cover all of the expenditures proposed, once they had reversed some of the cuts made previously, they would have to increase the property tax rate by more than the 9 cents that Interim Manager Ponder had originally proposed.

After this work session, school officials again stated they would seek mediation if this reduction was made and then, if necessary, go forward with litigation against the board. Superintendent Ed Sadler stated that "the schools can't afford to receive less than the $29 million they got this year from the county because of a $1.6 million increase in state-mandated teacher salaries and rising utility costs." After hearing from public safety agencies the day after this work session, several commissioners were quoted as saying they would consider changing their minds on the 5% cuts for public safety. Thus, the budget was far from being settled as the board prepared to meet during the last week of the budget cycle. In work sessions leading up to the final week, the board continued to debate the percentages they believed department budgets should be cut while also debating exceptions to percentage reductions. No consensus on how to balance the budget was apparent before the commissioners' final budget work session.

❖ AFTERMATH

After five hours of discussion during their final budget work session, the county commissioners passed, by a 4 to 3 vote, an increase in the property tax rate of 9.33 cents. This increase was larger than the 9-cent increase originally proposed by the interim county manager. Commissioner Price, who generally voted with Jenkins, Loftis, and Wright on reduction measures, aligned himself with the pro-tax-increase commissioners Keigher, Floyd, and Carpenter for this one vote. Commissioner Carpenter stated that the tax rate should have been increased three years earlier instead of using the county's fund balance to make up the operating budget's deficits. The tax hike made up about half of the $20.2 million shortfall with the rest being erased through decreases in the requested budgets of county agencies and departments. The public safety departments were spared major cuts of which the most noticeable were the 13 positions that had been proposed for elimination in the Gaston County Police Department. The school system was spared any reductions and received the same amount they were budgeted for fiscal year 2001. There was no further discussion of consolidating police functions. The only action taken on the hospital was to appoint a commission to study how the process would work if the board decided to sell this asset.

In summary, after the commissioners rejected the 9-cent property tax increase proposal of the interim manager, they ended up passing a budget with an increased tax level that slightly exceeded the interim manager's recommendation after strong lobbying by the affected parties. With the increase of 9.33 cents per $100 of assessed value, a property owner with a $100,000 home would see his or her tax bill rise from $825 to $918.30 annually for an 11.3% increase.

In early June 2001, the deputy county manager left to take a position in one of the state's larger cities. On July 6, 2001, Governor Easley announced that he would release $95 million in local government reimbursement money he had withheld earlier in the year. Gaston County's share of this money was almost $2 million. Interim County Manager Ponder announced that he would recommend that the county put this money in reserve in the county budget fund balance. What would you recommend the county do with the $2 million if you were a county commissioner?

2

Emergency Management at the Millennium

The Role of Information Systems

Maureen Brown

911:      911 Emergency, do you need police, fire, or medic?

Caller: [small child crying] My mommy and daddy are having a fight!

911:      Is he hitting her?

Caller: What? . . . Stop it! Mommy! Stop it! Don't hurt the baby! Stop it! . . . Would you just send the police, please?

911:      OK, we're going to be there. Who is hurting the baby?

Caller: Stop it! [crying]

911:      Where is your mom?

Caller: What?

911:      What's going on?

Caller: They are having a fight because . . . this has been going on forever and ever. . . . They always have this because he has a cousin and he is always drinking beer and getting drunk

Caller: He is hurting mommy! [crying]

911:      Don't cry, we are going to send the police.

Caller: OK.

911:      What is going on now?

Caller: He is trying to take the baby. . . . he is drunk, my stepdaddy is drunk! I think he is going to do something to the baby . . . [screaming, crying] He just knocked my little sister out, the 4-year-old, he pushed her down on the floor. . . . He just slapped mommy. . . . Oh my GOD! PLEASE SEND THE POLICE! [hang up]

911:      S—t.

A city's emergency call center is the primary lifeline for help in emergencies. The ability to respond quickly and effectively to emergency calls ranks as the highest priority for any city government and its citizens. And so it was for the City of San Benedictine (pseudonym for an actual U.S. city) at the turn of the last century.

❖ THE CITY

San Benedictine is a large urban city ranking 25th in size by population in the United States. In 1999, the population within the city boundaries reached 550,000, the population within the county boundaries approached 625,000, while the metropolitan statistical area (MSA) totaled 1.5 million. Population growth within both the city and the MSA had been robust and projections indicated that the city would grow 30% over the next 10 years. The booming economy and its resulting rapid growth rate had created many of the typical public administration problems. Service requests grew at a faster rate than city staff could accommodate, and the confusion that accompanied escalating production demands was evident throughout the city.

In large part because of its rapid growth rate, the strains of information collection, storage, and distribution in each of the city's departments escalated as well. The previous chief information officer (CIO) lacked the managerial and technical skills required to meet the various department needs, expectations, and desires. Given the management problems of the CIO, the city's information technology (IT) staff experienced a high degree of turnover, poor morale, and an inability to keep up with basic tasks. As a consequence, IT initiatives had become very decentralized. Each department established its own IT support staff, because the departments felt they could not rely on the city's IT department to meet their needs. The CIO had managed the majority of the city's projects poorly and the city manager had lost confidence in his ability to steer the city into the next century. Recognizing the problems, the city manager began to take the necessary actions required to remove the CIO and hire a replacement.

❖ THE METROPOLITAN POLICE DEPARTMENT

At the same time, a major reorganization was occurring in the police department. In 1993, the city council and county commissioners of the city and county of San Benedictine agreed to consolidate the city police department with the county police department to form the Metropolitan Police Department, under the direction of the city manager. This newly formed Metro Police Department (MPD) provided all law enforcement services to the city and the unincorporated areas of the county. In early 1994, the city hired a new police chief, Durwood Marwick, to integrate the two separate police departments into one united force and to continue implementing community policing and community-oriented problem solving throughout San Benedictine County.

Chief Marwick came to the city with extensive police experience. He had also served as the director of the state's Justice Information Services Division and as a result, was very knowledgeable about information and computer technology. Chief Marwick recognized the importance of data and information for the officers in the department to solve community problems. He further recognized that the information systems available in the MPD were not suited to support field officers. Consequently, he set out to build a cutting-edge information system to provide officers in the field with the information they needed to address crime-related problems.

Chief Marwick was aware of a new funding program that was being launched by the U.S. Department of Justice. Recognizing the antiquated computing environment that characterized most police departments, the new Clinton-Gore administration launched a major initiative to provide funding for new police systems. The COPS-MORE program provided funding for computer technology that would make officers more productive in the field and support community policing. Chief Marwick intended to take advantage of the funding opportunity and began to formulate plans for moving the MPD into the computer age.

The Police Department Builds Internal Information Capacities

One of the first steps the new chief took was to assign a police major to steer the IT initiatives. A needs analysis was conducted and a strategic information system plan was developed. Although widely accepted that information provides the foundation for community policing, the needs analysis revealed that officers lacked the requisite information and technologies required to address community policing needs in any effective manner. In short, the report identified that 75 to 80% of the officers felt uninformed on crime and suspect information and 90% claimed they had no information on residents who had been victimized. It became clearly evident to Chief Marwick that community policing could not be achieved without the supporting information systems.

In 1996, the chief presented his strategic information system plan to the city council with the strong support of the city manager. After hearing the chief's research and reasoning for new information systems, the city council overwhelmingly approved and authorized the MPD to establish information systems and the infrastructure to advance community-oriented problem solving pursuant to the strategic information system plan.

The chief moved quickly on the implementation of his community policing information systems. Taking advantage of the COPS-MORE program, the police department acquired $12.5 million in federal grants. The chief combined the grant funds with technology budget allocations from the city, MPD's operating budget, and other funding sources available to the chief, such as state block grants and drug asset forfeiture funds. The IT funding pool swelled to nearly $30 million, compared with the $110 million total operating budget for MPD in 1996. Knowing the problems of the current city CIO, Chief Marwick hired his own computer technology staff to handle the IT needs of the police.

At the same time that the chief was leveraging funding opportunities and building IT capacities in the police department, several other city departments were experiencing expensive IT project failures. Feeling the burden of the problems that many of the other departments experienced, the city manager mentioned to the chief, "It is such a relief to know that your department has the talent on board to take care of your IT needs and that you are doing the right things in the right way!"

Although the city manager was very comfortable with the IT developments in the police department, the relationship between the MPD computer staff and the city IT staff had become very contentious. Frustrated with all the problems in the city, many of the more talented city IT engineers requested transfers to the MPD. Considerable "brain drain" occurred, leaving the city IT department completely incapable of addressing even the most basic needs. In addition, funding resources and strong technical and leadership capacities allowed the MPD to excel while the other departments struggled with their IT initiatives. The MPD took the lead among all city departments in the implementation of its own IT systems, and the efforts were envied by many. However, the chief liked the decentralized arrangement. He would often state that his department was not only the largest department in the city—composing more than one-third of all city personnel—but that it also required technical support 24 hours a day. Hence, having internal IT support staff was absolutely necessary. The city manager agreed, and Chief Marwick built a highly skilled, well-rewarded IT team capable of migrating the department to a new technology platform.

The Heart of Police Systems: The CAD System

The police department's computer-aided dispatch (CAD) system was the heart of virtually all police work. In short, when a citizen called 911 with a problem, the address, nature of the incident, and other pertinent information were entered into the CAD. All the 911 calls for emergency services, such as police, fire, and ambulance, were answered by up to fifteen telecommunicators in a central communications center located within the police department. A telecommunicator answered 911 calls from scared, angry, upset people who needed emergency services. The telecommunicator entered the information into the CAD and in less than a second, the computer presented the call for service to the appropriate dispatcher, who then alerted the next available emergency unit by radio. The call data were forwarded to the officer's laptop in the car, and the officer added additional information to the incident record. The MPD had been dispatching emergency calls for service in this way for 24 years virtually without fail. Since 1988, the call-for-service data were also sent over a wireless data system to the field unit's vehicle-mounted mobile data terminal or, more recently, the laptop computer.

In the event the CAD system failed, a backup system involved recording the essential data from 911 calls for service on long slender 3.5" × 8" cards. Once the telecommunicators recorded the critical information on the card, they would physically stand up and walk several steps to a table with large tablets of computer printouts of all the street addresses in the county. They would check the appropriate tablet and locate the street name and block number for the call for service to determine the precise geographic location of the call. They then entered that sector on the card and hand-delivered it to the appropriate radio dispatcher within the Communications Center. Since the manual process could take five to ten minutes longer than the automated process, the thought of going "all manual" on a busy night was something that "struck fear and terror into the hearts" of all telecommunicators and dispatchers.

With the CAD in operation, a staff of 15 telecommunicators could handle between 200 to 300 calls per hour with ease. In manual mode, that number dropped to under 100 before calls were "dropped" or missed entirely. This meant that a heart attack victim would not get his ambulance in time, or an elderly woman would not get the fire department to her house before she was overcome by smoke and the house engulfed in flames. The thought of someone being injured or dying because of an unwarranted delay was something that dispatchers feared most. "I don't ever want it to happen on my shift, I just couldn't live with it. I am responsible for getting these cars out quickly; people's lives depend on me."

Virtually every work unit in the department depended on the data that originated in the CAD system. The current CAD was placed into full operation in 1975. At that time the City of San Benedictine had a population of 277,000, a service area of 105 square miles, and answered 146,000 calls for service annually. By 1997, the police department served a population of 620,000 spread over 525 square miles and answered 608,000 calls for service annually.

The CAD ran on an IBM mainframe computer, which was the state-of-the-art architecture in 1975. Gayle, the COBOL programmer who worked on the CAD system in the mid-1970s during its development, was still on MPD staff. Gayle had handled all changes and modifications made to the system since 1975. She had virtually every line of the nearly 2 million lines of program code memorized. She knew the table structures, interfaces, interdependencies, and strengths and weaknesses of the system. She was a perfectionist. In addition, Gayle had the support of Larry, who understood the IBM mainframe on which the CAD code ran. The two of them made an excellent support team for the CAD system. The MPD was fortunate to still have Gayle on staff until the new CAD system was installed, and Larry to support the hardware. Gayle was so married to the CAD system that she planned to retire when the MPD replaced "her" CAD system, which was planned for late 1999.

Although the 1975 CAD code had served the MPD well, everyone acknowledged that system limitations conflicted with the community policing paradigm. The 1975 system was very limited in its ability to capture the critical data that officers required to engage in community-oriented problem solving. The system could not provide officers with the history of an address. So, when responding to a call, officers were not able to determine if other officers had been to the residence once or multiple times for the same event. The CAD could not track officer time in the field so it could not assist with resource deployment strategies or permit strategic call management. The CAD could not provide timely ad hoc reports that allowed the officers to provide feedback on service and crime events in the field. The CAD simply could not support the information-intensive needs of community policing and problem solving. In fact, it actually impeded the implementation of community-oriented problem solving by forcing the officers to continue to operate according to a model that no longer proved fruitful. The aging CAD system was in need of upgrading, but city funding limitations in the past had prevented its replacement.

Ideally, given the COPS-MORE funding, and Chief Marwick's plans to upgrade MPD's information systems, the new CAD system would be purchased and implemented before 2000 to avoid any problems that might be experienced from the year 2000 (Y2K) computer defect (see Box 2.1). The new CAD system would capture the data required for community policing and problem solving and provide the data in a manner that enabled officers to develop and implement appropriate community problem-solving strategies. The new system would collect information on all patrol officer activities to allow the department to develop accurate resource deployment strategies to maximize the amount of time officers were engaged in community problem solving. It was hoped that through the call management strategies provided from the new CAD, citizens would experience a much higher level of satisfaction with the services of the MPD.

Box 2.1

The Year 2000 problem (also known as Y2K, millennium bug, or millennium virus) stems from the so-called "early years" of computer programming when every keystroke was critical. To save time and costly memory space the vast majority of early computer programmers identified years only by their last two digits thereby taking for granted that the first two digits of each year would be "19." As a result, programming practices evolved around the use of six-digit dates (dd/mm/yy) as opposed to eight-digit dates (dd/mm/yyyy). The root of the problem arises when a computer program attempts to read the date "00." This could mean either "2000" or "1900." Hence, any computer program that deals with six-digit codes was susceptible to the Y2K problem.

The pivotal problems of the Y2K issue really center on three key problem areas: date mathematics, date validity tests, and programmable logic devices. Although the problem itself is not terribly complicated, the potential implications of the issue are far-reaching and therefore these three areas need to be examined in some detail.

Date Mathematics. For years businesses have relied on date math to compute things such as aging schedules, due dates, past due accounts, etc., and many of the most heavily used computer applications have been created to support the use of such calculations

(Lotus 1-2-3, MS-Excel, MS-Access). These applications all work by simply using a base year (often Jan. 1, 1900) as a starting point and then tracking the date and time numerically from that point to see how much time has elapsed. In order to do this, the program often reads time as a fractional representation of the day integer. MS-Excel, for example, reads May 12, 1998, 3:08 p.m. as 35927.63 (or number of days elapsed since Jan. 01, 1900). With this formula, one could compute the difference between today and when a bill was incurred and the resulting number would indicate how old the particular debt was (35927-35882 = 45 days past due).

This is where the Y2K problem factors into the situation. By using six-digit dates, the computer could possibly misinterpret 01/01/00 as the year 1900 and therefore 01/01/00 − 05/12/98 would result in a large negative number (in this case 35926). Although this number may be an issue the computer application can deal with, the potential problems are numerous. For example, in this case the large negative number could be converted into the absolute value, because the negative sign is dropped if no space is reserved to hold it. One could imagine the confusion if their debt went from 22 days old to 35,926 days old. The past due notice would be quite a surprise, and if this debt was further coupled with compounded interest calculations the potential chain reaction could be enormous.

Date Validity Testing. The second type of problem involves systems that check the date for some purpose to determine if a valid date is being used. A simple example of this might be found with a credit card expiration date validation test. It is possible that the program that validates the expiration date, once the card is scanned, might read 01/01/99 as greater than 01/01/00 and therefore reject the credit card. The potential for larger problems should be evident here. Another example of this is a security system that checks to see if today is a valid date before recording an entry or exit from a building. If the 00 date is determined to be out of range or the computation is at fault, the system may simply shut down and lock all the doors.

Programmable Logic Devices. Finally, the term programmable logic devices (PLDs) is used to refer to the many semiconductor-based "chips" that manage various devices. These include anything from simple coffee machines to large production and manufacturing machines, and it is estimated that literally tens of billions of them exist around the world. These devices are usually programmed using Assembler programming language and often contain date-sensitive code that is not set up to receive eight-digit dates. The potential problems here include anything from VCR recording failures to major power plant failures.

Contract Initiatives

The MPD was determined that the Y2K computer bug would not disrupt their mission-critical CAD system; too much was at stake for the city to allow that to happen. Not only was it completely unacceptable for the CAD system to become nonfunctional at the turn of the century, but given concerns over the potential deleterious impact of the Y2K defect, the city was to undertake a disaster preparedness plan that would go into effect on New Year's Eve (see Box 2.2). The police had to prepare for the worst-case scenario: an avalanche of calls resulting from widespread system failures and the resulting public panic. Fire, medical, and police calls could not be dropped, missed, or lost. Knowing the criticality of the CAD system to delivering emergency services, the police department sought to replace the old system and issued a request for proposals for a new CAD system in February 1998.

Box 2.2   Thousands Will Be Poised for Disaster Dec. 31

By Jason Hagey
Tri-City Herald staff writer

Amid all the questions about the Year 2000 computer problem, one thing is certain: It will be one of the biggest killjoys of all time.

Instead of partying like it's 1999, as the singer formerly known as Prince has been exhorting us to do for years, New Year's Eve 1999 will find thousands of people at work, poised for a disaster that may or may not happen.

(Text continues on page 27)

Police officers will be on the beat, firefighters and paramedics on standby in case the world's computers crash at the stroke of midnight, plunging the world into darkness and anarchy. A Texas hospital plans to have a doctor or nurse beside every occupied bed in the building, just in case. Manufacturing executives who would normally be away on ski vacations will be at their factories, keeping a watch over their fortunes.

Bankers will be watching account balances. Utility workers will be on alert. And journalists will be out in the streets with cameras and notebooks, ready to document whatever happens.

It doesn't matter that what happens could be nothing.

The infamous millennium bug, or Y2K problem as it is commonly called, was created more than 30 years ago by pioneer computer programmers. In an effort to save scarce and expensive space on computer hard drives, the programmers elected to adopt a shorthand when referring to the date. Instead of programming a computer to read July 1, 1970, as 07-01-1970, for example, it was instructed to read it as simply 07-01-70.

For decades, the decision was of little or no consequence, but with the coming rollover of the calendar it has become hugely significant. Instead of interpreting the year 00 as 2000, the fear is that computers will be tricked into thinking it is 1900.

If that happens, no one can say what might result. Some computers might shut down. Others might malfunction.

"To be realistic, nobody can predict exactly to what degree Y2K will impact each one of us," said Larry Gerhardstein, a senior research scientist at the Pacific Northwest National Laboratory in Richland. "Realistically, nobody knows."

Uncertainty about the extent of the problem, and fear it will shut down enough computers to trigger a chain reaction capable of seizing the world's infrastructure, has replaced the Cold War as America's No. 1 reason to worry about the end of the world.

Stories about survivalists building stockpiles of food and ammunition in preparation for a computer-driven apocalypse started showing up with regularity in the media during the last year.

Gradually the news stories have given way to more serious accounts of people worrying about Y2K, and taking steps to prepare for it.

The fact that the problem is potentially so serious demonstrates just how ubiquitous computers have become. Indeed, computers control just about every aspect of modern life, from the electricity that comes out of our wall sockets and the water that flows from our taps to the cash that spits out of our bank machines.

Adding to the problem is the fact that so-called embedded chips—some of which are programmed to read calendar dates—are inside all sorts of products people don't normally think of as being computers.

Modern appliances and machines, from car engines and robots used in manufacturing to VCRs and coffee makers, are liable to have embedded chips inside them controlling some part of their operation.

Not all of the chips will fail, of course. Experts say only a small number of them are likely to be affected by the date change at all.

The problem is figuring out which ones are susceptible—and when. For one thing, it isn't always apparent which products are likely to contain chips that keep track of the calendar. Devices like VCRs, which can be programmed to record programs at a set time on a set day, obviously keep track of the calendar, but even some products that don't need to have calendar-sensitive chips contain them.

Why? The reason, according to Maryland consultant Mark Frautschi, is economics. It's often cheaper for manufacturers to buy off-the-shelf chips with calendars built-in than to design systems specifically for their product, Frautschi explained.

And just because a product keeps working on Jan. 1, 2000 isn't always a guarantee it's not Y2K sensitive, either. If it contains a chip with an internal clock that only advances when the device is turned on, it might take several years beyond 2000 for the internal clock to reach 2000, Frautschi said.

Coming to terms with the Y2K problem, psychologists have observed, can lead to the same range of emotions as finding out about a terminal illness or coping with the death of a loved one.

Denial is often the first response, followed by anger, fear, depression and panic, and ending in acceptance and cooperation. Gloria Woodward, who teaches classes in Kennewick on food storage and preparation, has watched her class sizes soar from about 10 or 12 people to nearly 50 people as people in the Tri-Cities reach the panic and acceptance stages.

She expects the numbers to climb even more as the year progresses.

Customers are coming to her in search of hand flour mills, storage containers and advice on how to prepare food without electricity.

Many of them are in a sort of "measured panic" state, Woodward said, as they brace for the possibility of life without electricity.

Woodward herself is only slightly worried about Y2K. As a Mormon, she has always practiced food storage and therefore has needed only to update and complete her usual supply.

She isn't taking a bunker mentality, but she will be ready. It could even be a good thing in one respect, she said, if it forces people to think less of themselves and more of others.

"It if happens like some people say it's going to happen, I hope people pull together and work together to get through it," Woodward said.

A small but growing number of mostly left-leaning people are saying the same thing.

Y2K, they suggest, might very well be the end of the world as we know it.

But it might also be one of the best things that could happen to the world.

In this scenario, cul-de-sacs where neighbors pass each other in their SUVs without ever saying hello will be transformed into close-knit communities where members are forced to rely on each other for the basics of life.

"As we prepare for Y2K, something surprising and quite wonderful is going to happen," Eric Utne, founder of Utne Reader, is quoted as saying on the cover of the Y2K Citizen's Action Guide. "We're going to get to know our neighbors."

Still, others remain skeptical.

Could it be that the concern over Y2K is nothing more than a fantastic boon for computer programmers, civil attorneys, crackpot survivalists and sensational journalists?

"I think people are overreacting," said Ira Schmidt, director of information services at Columbia Basin College.

In fact, most government agencies discussing Y2K have adopted a strategy of alerting people about the potential problem, but trying not to induce panic.

"From all indications at this juncture, it's going to be a non-event," Bob Noland, the city of Kennewick's finance manager, told the city council recently.

The city, nevertheless, is suggesting people prepare for a Y2K power outage the same way they would prepare for an ice storm.

There are other small but important steps people can take to prepare.

Schmidt, for example, recommends keeping paper records of things like bank accounts and credit card statements in case of mistakes. Outrageous bills and unwarranted penalties are possibilities, he said.

But he isn't worried about large-scale problems.

And neither is Gerhardstein, who has spent the last year working with electric utilities to prepare for the Y2K problem.

There isn't enough time left to fix everything, Gerhardstein said, but most of the important things should work with little or no trouble, including electricity.

For his part, Gerhardstein plans on spending New Year's Eve at home watching television, just like normal.

"I am definitely not a doomsdayer," Gerhardstein said, adding, "There are a lot of those out there."

The tide of public and expert opinion now seems to come down somewhere in the middle, with most people believing Y2K will neither pass completely unnoticed, nor will it bring about the end of the world.

Sen. Bob Bennett, chairman of the Senate's Y2K committee, exemplifies the federal government's attempt to find a middle ground.

"We must recognize that this problem is coming and that it must be dealt with coldly, intelligently, and efficiently," Bennett, R-Utah, said last June. "Don't panic, but don't spend a lot of time sleeping either."

Or partying. Unless it's at work.

Tri-City Herald, Kennewick, WA. Thousands will be poised for disaster Dec. 31st, by Jason Hagey. Reprinted with permission.

The plan was to have a new system in place and fully operational by the end of 1999. However, because of the critical nature of the system, a backup plan was also devised and steps were taken to modify the 1975 CAD programs as necessary to enable the older system to function into the year 2000 if needed.

After studying the issue, Gayle and Larry recommended that a minimalist remediation effort could be put in place to patch the old system in the event that it was needed. The recommendation was to actually forego expanding the year field from two to four digits. They saw expanding the date field as a high-risk procedure that would place the system in jeopardy of total failure. The code had been revised multiple times in the 24 years it had been in operation, so the modification required to expand the date field was reasonably likely to result in a number of cascading problems that might lead to an inoperable system. Because the CAD system did not require any calculations on the year, the two-digit field was viewed as an acceptable short-term solution if the system was needed at the turn of the century. They estimated that the work involved to remediate the old system was not extensive—they anticipated that it might take two to three weeks to make changes in the code. The minor changes would allow the system to log and dispatch 911 emergency calls but did not provide for much else. The police department and the city regarded the minimalist approach offered by Gayle and Larry as especially attractive as a backup plan. The MPD did not want to invest any more public dollars in an old CAD system. At the same time the request for proposals (RFP) for a new CAD system was released and hopes were high that the new system would be operational before January 1, 2000.

During spring 1998 the city hired a new CIO. The new CIO came from a neighboring city with a slightly smaller population, but with many of the same growth problems experienced by San Benedictine. He had a good track record and a personality that was open and friendly. The city manager had included all of the various city department heads in the final stages of the selection process to allow the department heads to meet the final candidates and to get buy-in for her final selection. Although the new CIO hit it off well with the department heads initially, it became apparent to them that the friendly new CIO was intent on recentralizing most computer-related functions under city control. The department heads had gotten accustomed to having their own computer services in-house. They saw the CIO's efforts to centralize similar computer functions as threatening and an attempt to rob them of control over the systems they felt were critical to their operations. Under this perception the CIO's honeymoon with the department heads came to an end, and the department heads took a defensive posture. However, the city manager had a lot of faith and confidence in the new CIO. Consequently, the CIO gradually won battles with the various departments; hardware and software standards were imposed, and joint management with city IT of major IT projects in the departments was required.

Among the CIO's many responsibilities, addressing the Y2K software defect loomed large. After his arrival, he immediately launched a citywide Y2K preparedness initiative. All of the city's executive team attended the project kickoff meeting. The purpose of the meeting was to determine the scope of the Y2K remediation effort and to determine how it could be funded with the current resource base. The city had $7 million available, but early analyses indicated that the city might require up to $20 million to remediate all the systems in operation at the time. The meeting was highly contentious in nature, the assistant city manager was clearly concerned about the budget shortfall, the potential for disaster in the critical city systems, and the quickly approaching December 31, 1999, deadline. Among the many systems in operation, CAD, utility billing, payroll, budgeting, and finance were seen as critical systems that must be remediated for Y2K; none of these systems could afford a political, functional, or financial failure.

Visions of the national media focusing on the calamity resulting from nonremediated or failed systems served to heighten the stress level and fears of the city executive team. Adding to the tension was the knowledge, or fear, that widespread system failures would lead to panic and therefore heighten the need for police, fire, and medical requests for assistance. Industry experts varied widely on their predictions of the full impact of the Y2K problem. Some experts forecasted a complete social, political, and economic crash; others were less pessimistic but nonetheless equally concerned.

❖ DISASTER LOOMS LARGE

The fear of city collapse weighed heavily on the city's new CIO. Television talk shows, newspaper articles, and news reports focused intently on the potential disasters that could result and recommended that citizens take extra measures to protect themselves from the failures that might occur. The simplest measures proposed focused on storing water, canned goods, and cash. Others recommended constructing emergency shelters equipped with enough supplies to last several months. Fear was running high, and those in positions of authority and responsibility felt the pressure of the widespread fear.

The CIO was designated by the city manager to make the Y2K project succeed and was under tremendous emotional pressure to successfully remediate these critical systems. He had a clear sense of responsibility, and that his job, as well as the city manager's job, were at stake. Recognizing that the total Y2K effort had a cost estimate of $20 million and that the city only had $7 million available, the city executive team was faced with some very difficult decisions. Decisions had to be made on how to allocate the dollars that were available for remediating only those systems that were perceived as mission critical.

Other systems would have to go unremediated. If widespread system failures occurred in non-mission-critical systems, it was hoped that council members, the media, and the citizens would be patient with the interference in services.

Given that Gayle and Larry felt that the CAD system was not in any jeopardy of failure from the Y2K bug and that efforts were under way to purchase a new system, the chief offered to relinquish the $1 million the city had set aside for remediating the old CAD. Feeling confident that Gayle's code would run, the police department's staff felt that the situation was well under control, and that the funds were not needed and could be better used for remediating other city systems. Understanding that the police had to be prepared to handle the escalation in calls and ensuing panic that would occur if the community's systems failed, the police remained confident in their plans and felt that the situation was under control. The city executive team was delighted to hear that the police department had a Y2K plan in place, and that progress had been made and that the $1 million was not needed. Everyone agreed with the police department plan. Gayle and Larry were notified to continue to remediate the current CAD system to keep it functional in 2000 without significant changes to the code's file structure.

New Replacement for CAD System

By May 1998, the proposals arrived in response to the RFP for the implementation of the new CAD system. During the next six weeks a committee of end users and technical staff evaluated the proposals and identified the system that could meet police, fire, and EMS needs. Plans were well under way to select a product and execute a contract with the new CAD vendor. One of the most startling revelations for the selection committee was the lack of products available from which to choose. Given the small market, off-the-shelf software systems for government operations did not tend to attract private-sector developers.

The CAD vendor that was selected had installed its software at a number of localities throughout the United States as well as Europe. The CAD system was believed to be the best system on the market. The gap between the selected vendor's product and the runner-up was tremendous; the runner-up system was basically unacceptable. All the users of the chosen vendor's CAD system gave the system rave reviews. The MPD staff was anxious to get the new system installed. MPD management saw the new system as a solution to many of its problems as well. The new system would provide better data on the activities of officers. Crime problems and repeat calls for service could be identified and resolved and officers could be held accountable for their activities. Excessive "out of service" time could be monitored and high performance could be rewarded.

During this same period the city selected a contractor to remediate the city's utility billing, payroll, budgeting, and finance systems for the Y2K defect. The company was a well-known firm with business conducted worldwide. However, the city's Y2K project was the first assignment with this company and for the newly hired project manager. His background was in the aerospace industry and his project management experience related to building aircraft. This Y2K project was his first exposure to managing a computer technology project. His remediation team was a collection of individuals hired for their apparent knowledge and experience in COBOL programming. They had not worked together before, were brought together for this project only, and would be released after the project was completed. The MPD staff had no input into the language of the contract between the city and the contractor.

Noting that the CAD system was not identified for remediation, the contractor offered to conduct a free independent review of the MPD's CAD code. The offer by the contractor was not to test system functionality, but rather to perform a cursory search for the presence of all the date fields in the code. Although the police department felt confident in Gayle's knowledge of where the date fields existed and her abilities to remediate, given the criticality of the system, and because the test was offered at no cost, the MPD decided to take advantage of the opportunity and agreed to allow the vendor to test the code as a preventive measure. In actuality, the MPD did not have much say in this decision. The decision was political—if the contractor would perform the test for free, the city and police department had no choice but to agree, or else risk a publicity frenzy that might occur if the news media caught wind of the fact that the police department refused to allow the city's Y2K contract vendor to test the code at no cost. But, at the time, it was of no real concern because the MPD management believed and felt confident that the new CAD system would be in place by November 1999. In addition, MPD management recognized that Gayle and Larry's remediation efforts were well under way as a backup strategy.

New CAD Dims

After three months of contract development efforts, negotiations with the vendor of the new CAD system began to break down during the fall of 1998. During the contract process, the MPD insisted that certain features be available on the new system. The vendor claimed that the features would require additional work and hence, increase the scope of the effort and cost of the system. Although the police argued that these features were included in the RFP and that the vendor stated in the RFP that they could provide the features at the quoted price, the vendor claimed that they "noted the request for the features" but did not actually agree to provide them. Both the police and the vendor were well aware of the Y2K problem and the fact that the police needed implementation before 2000. The price of the new CAD system had skyrocketed from the original estimate the vendor provided of $1.4 million to $2.7 million. The contract negotiations became very heated. The police department found itself in a predicament. The vendor was demanding more than the MPD could afford, and there was no time to go out to conduct another call for proposals. As complicating factors, the fear of calamity at the turn of the century loomed large, and the vendor had been especially effective at creating divisiveness within the police team. Several of the police members were risk-averse and felt it necessary to give the vendor whatever it requested as long as the new CAD would be installed on time. Others saw the vendor as exploiting the police department's vulnerability at a critical time for personal gain. An impasse had clearly occurred. The conversations became extremely heated among the police department's staff.

Further meetings were held with Gayle and Larry regarding their confidence level in the 1975 CAD code. More tests were run and the code continued to perform well even when the computer's clock was set at different dates in the year 2000. As further assurance, Gayle and Larry set the clock at 11:55 p.m. on December 31, 1999, and watched to see what would happen with the system when the clock rolled over. The system continued to hum along without any interruptions. Given this reassurance, the police department decided not to agree to the vendor's demands and announced internally that the new system would not be up and running as originally planned. The decision had been made to forego the opportunity to have a new CAD system operational by the end of 1999.

The Countdown Begins

In early spring 1999, Chief Marwick, to the surprise of the entire city, resigned. A temporary acting chief was installed until a replacement could be recruited. Recognizing that he was in a temporary, undesirable position, the acting chief's management philosophy was to take a minimalist approach and to avoid any controversial issues. He sought to maintain a status quo position until a new chief was selected.

In late spring, IBM announced that it was upgrading several of its compilers (a program that converts programming code into machine-readable language) and would no longer support the version of the compiler that Gayle's code required. The police department did not anticipate the announcement and was caught off guard. After several phone calls, the police department found a vendor that agreed to provide support for the compiler. Apparently, the vendor had staff on board that knew the compiler code very well and was willing to enter into a contract arrangement to support the compiler Gayle's code required for the year 2000. The city executive team was notified of IBM's decision to upgrade and the fact that the police department found a third party to support the compiler.

By June, the city's remediation contractor was nearing completion of remediation on the various different city systems and began testing Gayle's CAD software. The results indicated that in the two million lines of code there were 523 date fields that were two digits in size. The contractor told the city staff that they did not have any confidence that the system would run at the turn of the century. "Furthermore," stated the contractor's report, "the '75 CAD code runs on a compiler that IBM will no longer support." The police department's response to the report was that the contractor looked specifically for two-digit years that the police department conceded existed (in fact they deliberately did not change them). The police department had tested whether the system would actually operate after January 1, 2000, and did not encounter problems with the two-digit date field. Because the remediation strategy allowed for the retention of the two-digit year, any test that searched for two-digit years would find them. The fact that the system continued with two-digit year fields did not affect the functioning of the system. In addition, although it was true that IBM would no longer support the compiler, a contract had already been entered into with a third party for support of the compiler.

However, the city's Y2K contractor would not "certify" the CAD code as being Y2K compliant (and thereby relieve the city of potential liability for failure of the system), and the responsibilities for the risk of a nonperforming CAD system was placed squarely on the shoulders of the city. Police testing of the system continued to support the findings that the CAD would run just fine in the new century. Yet, given escalating media coverage of the Y2K fallout and ever-increasing levels of fear, the city executives had become uncomfortable with not having a vendor certification that the CAD system was fully Y2K compliant.

The contractor offered to remediate the police department's code over the next five months at a cost of $2 million. The city's CIO was delighted, and the police department was outraged. The police department perceived the initiative as totally unnecessary and wasteful spending, as well as price gouging by the city's Y2K remediation contractor. Moreover, they were terrified by the prospect of a third party altering Gayle's code, a complex system of two million lines that only Gayle understood. To the police department, tampering with the code meant putting the community at higher risk for unacceptably long response times for police, fire, and EMS service.

❖ WEIGHING THE RISKS: A QUESTION OF LIABILITY

The police department felt that the riskier route was to turn the CAD code over to the contractor and allow its staff to attempt to remediate the code within the remaining five months. Adding to the problem was the fact that, if the date field was expanded from two to four digits, all the connections with the external systems required modification, so the choice of falling back on the old code was no longer an option as it would not work with the newly modified connections. In essence, agreement to remediate meant that there was no safety net. If the contractor was not able to meet the deadline, there would be no CAD in place at the turn of the century and the telecommunicators would have to dispatch via manual mode.

Although the city agreed that the remaining five months of 1999 did not provide sufficient time for remediation, and that it would be difficult to be successful within five months, the city was not willing to assume the potential liability associated with the 1975 code. To add insult to injury, because the city no longer had any remediation funds left to fund this $2 million project to remediate and certify the CAD code, the police department was ordered by the city manager to finance the project out of its operational budget.

The police technical team pleaded with the acting chief to intervene strongly against this decision. In the meeting Gayle voiced her concerns about the complexity of the code and the ability of the contractor to successfully remediate the code at all, much less in five months. She stated that, having worked with them on testing the system, she had no faith in the contractor. She felt so strongly about the contractor's inability to understand the code and to fix the CAD system in time that she announced that she would retire effective November 1, 1999, and she submitted a formal petition to be removed from the project. She felt that the city was placing the citizens and the officers at an unacceptably high level of risk without cause by agreeing to allow the contractor to tamper with the code that she had already proven to operate normally in the year 2000.

The following day the police department appealed to the city CIO to reconsider the city's plan to remediate the CAD system for $2 million. The police department staff voiced their concerns that the decision to remediate would actually place citizen safety at a greater risk if attempts were made to remediate in the remaining five months. There simply was not enough time, the code was too complex, and the 1975 code had been tested and was found to perform under year 2000 scenarios.

The CIO acknowledged that it would be very difficult for the contractor to remediate the CAD system in the five months, but that by pursuing the contract, responsibility for a functionally performing system became the contractor's responsibility, thereby protecting the city manager from criticism. Hence, the CAD system would be remediated and certified for $2 million. The acting chief remained silent throughout the meeting. When the issue was raised that the one person who understood the code, Gayle, refused to work on the project and planned to retire in protest, the CIO concluded the meeting by stating, "Let her retire, the contractor does not need her."

The next week the Clinton administration passed legislation to protect software vendors against liability as a result of their efforts to mitigate or prevent Y2K failures.

3

The Quest to Continue

Healthy Communities, Inc.[1]

Sherril B. Gelmon and Robert J. Gassner

❖ BACKGROUND

Healthy Communities, Inc. (HCI) was established in 1996 in the Portland, Oregon, metropolitan region to respond to an opportunity to develop and promote communitywide cooperation on community health improvement issues. Before the creation of HCI, numerous agencies were working simultaneously on issues such as teen pregnancy, domestic violence, homeless youth, alcohol and drug abuse, access to health services, and provision of dental care. At any one time, there might be 4 to 15 different agencies addressing the same problem but with no coordination of effort or communication regarding plans, actions, and progress. With the creation of HCI, a single neutral convener was created to serve as a coordinator, communicator, and facilitator of collaboration.

The actual triggering event for the creation of HCI was a national grant solicitation, for which a group of local health leaders decided to apply. HCI's mission, adopted by its board of directors in 1997 and reaffirmed in 2000, was "to help transform the way public and private groups in the three-county area address and share responsibility for community improvement." The mission was further elaborated by a set of strategies that operationalized the mission; these strategies were the following:

- Facilitate health-sector participation by fostering opportunities for health-related organizations to participate in community initiatives.
- Implement model projects using a collaborative community development approach through the implementation and continual assessment of selected projects and support.
- Serve as a regional resource and clearinghouse for information sharing and technical assistance on community health development and collaborations.
- Share what works by increasing the public awareness of successful projects and initiatives that advance the use of the collaborative community development approach.
- Be responsive to opportunities by actively responding to community needs and requests to facilitate projects based on the HCI model.

The organization's bylaws stated that its purpose was to improve the health of communities in the tricounty area through collaboration, education, facilitation, and other related activities. HCI was similar to other local efforts nationwide that grew out of the "Model Cities" (U.S.-based) initiative of the 1960s, and the "Healthy Cities" (international) initiatives of the 1970s and 1980s. In 2001, the "Healthy Communities" movement was a coordinated effort to improve the overall health of communities through participatory, community-driven collaborations.[2]

❖ GOVERNANCE

HCI was governed by a board of directors consisting of up to 12 members (see Appendix 3.1). Criteria for appointment to the board included willingness to serve; representation of a relevant constituent group; expertise and skills of value to HCI; potential to provide linkages and networks across the community; and fund-raising ability or connections. The overall board complement was also intended to represent demographic diversity of age, race, gender, and geography (across the three counties—Multnomah [urban], Washington [urban/rural], and Clackamas [urban/rural]). Board members were expected to attend board meetings, assume committee responsibilities, represent HCI at community events as appropriate, and raise or leverage funds to support HCI operations.

The board met monthly to review operations, discuss new opportunities, make resource decisions, and plan for the future. It elected its own officers to the positions of president, vice president, secretary, and treasurer. These four officers composed an executive committee, which met as needed between board meetings and had the authority to act on behalf of the board regarding urgent operational decisions.

There were eight members of the board in 2000 and four vacancies. Two board members had been involved with the board since the inception of the organization; another four had been on the board between two and four years; and two had joined the board during the past year. Two long-standing members of the board had resigned within the past year—one because of other commitments, and another because of relocation out of the area.

❖ STAFFING

The organization was staffed by three people: an executive director, a program coordinator, and an administrative assistant. The executive director provided overall leadership and direction for all activities of HCI and participated in community outreach work. The program coordinator did extensive community outreach work and some office administration. The administrative assistant answered the telephone, responded to inquiries, coordinated activities such as mail and photocopying, managed the Web site, and handled the bookkeeping.

HCI worked closely with the local universities and often had students participating in projects through special course projects, independent research activities, and formal field internships. Most of these students were graduate students in either a master's of public health program, with specialization in either health administration/policy or health education, or a master's of public administration program, often with a concentration in nonprofit management. There had also been students from time to time who were senior-level undergraduates seeking a community-based experience, or from nursing, medicine, or allied health fields.

❖ ACTIVITIES

As it operated, HCI identified important community health issues and then helped organize community solutions to these issues. This process was initiated through ongoing environmental scanning, conducted primarily by the executive director and the program coordinator. They accomplished this scanning by monitoring Web sites and the media, attending community and coalition meetings, tracking other community-based research and projects, and periodically meeting with a set of key community informants. HCI then convened meetings of key stakeholders interested in specific issues, conducted focused research on an issue, or facilitated discussions of existing groups to help them to identify issues.

After issues were identified, staff members developed position papers and made recommendations to the board, and the board deliberated and made decisions on which new initiatives to pursue. The staff could be very influential in these decisions, although there were some issues over the years that selected board members fought either strongly for or against.

The next step after issue selection was development of volunteer teams of people (known as "action teams" to clearly emphasize that action was expected and intended) from community, government, nonprofit, and private organizations that agreed to work together. Action teams usually had 10 to 15 members, with a designated chair appointed by the HCI board. The action teams, with support from HCI, attempted to improve coordination of various organizations' efforts or create capacity to develop new programs or services to address the issue. Past action teams achieved great success working to improve coordination of health services for homeless youth, provide dental care for low-income children, and establish prevention and treatment services for families dealing with head lice. Results of these efforts included a formalized coalition of local service providers focusing on homeless youth who subsequently received a multi-million-dollar federal grant to support their efforts; a state-supported dental sealant program for children; and a foundation-funded public resource center addressing issues related to head lice prevention and treatment. These three teams each completed their work with HCI and evolved into new or freestanding organizations.

In 2000, HCI was in the process of developing a new action team to address environmental health issues in a rural part of the tricounty metropolitan region. According to a recent state government report, the region was facing severe health challenges caused by rapid population growth and industrial development. This team had not yet been formally proposed to the board, pending further developmental activities.

Action teams worked on issues that the local communities had not yet addressed. Therefore, action teams had not been established to address common issues such as HIV/AIDS, teen pregnancy, welfare to work, health care access, or domestic violence as there already were active coalitions effectively addressing these issues in the tricounty area. HCI sought to be nonduplicative of other existing efforts. Over the years, there had been heated board discussions where one board member had a particular passion about an issue and wanted HCI to develop an action team, but other board members overruled such proposals based on existing community initiatives.

In all of its work, HCI stressed that its approach was as follows:

- Asset-based—recognizing and building on the strategies and expertise already available in the community
- Action-oriented—moving forward to implement specific strategies and projects
- Nonterritorial—facilitating the elimination of territorial or turf battles
- Multisectoral—involving people and organizations with varying purposes, resources, and points of view
- Multidisciplinary—addressing multiple factors that affect the health of the communities

The staff and board members believed HCI had an excellent reputation as an organization that helped other people and organizations solve problems. The comment heard most often was that "HCI's strength lay in its ability to serve as a neutral convener and facilitator with no vested interests," something that could not be said of many of the other similar community collaborations. (Approximately 15 had been identified that had interests and missions overlapping with those of HCI.) An article in the local newspaper, *The Portlander*, about the creation of the head lice resource center stated: "Healthy Communities, Inc., fills a void in this community by providing the leadership to attack important problems without any of the political agendas so often seen due to organizational mission, ownership, affiliation, or other value-laden characteristics of many of our most prominent community-based nonprofit organizations."

❖ RESOURCES

HCI was initially funded in part by a three-year grant from the Wheat Family Foundation as one of twenty-five sites across the country selected as pilot sites for Healthy Communities activities. Part of that grant required that HCI have matching funds. A local coalition of health care systems and health insurers, the Portland Collaborative (see Appendix 3.2 for membership), agreed to provide matching contributions. HCI operated for its first five years as a "program" of the Portland Collaborative. The Collaborative provided financial management services and legal status as a nonprofit corporation; the latter was essential in order for HCI to apply for certain grants. An "advisory committee" (the Collaborative's term) governed HCI—but in fact it operated as a board of directors.

By 2000, the HCI had evolved with interests and goals that diverged from those of the Collaborative. The HCI's advisory committee decided to become an independent organization and apply for 501(c)(3) tax-exempt status. The Collaborative approved this independence, and its members agreed to continue to provide funding for another two years to help HCI become established. The advisory committee transitioned into the current HCI board of directors with no immediate change in its membership.

HCI rented office space in a building housing a number of community-based nonprofit organizations. HCI had access to the building's office support equipment, such as photocopiers, as well as conference rooms and larger spaces for public meetings at no additional charge. Office furnishings and computers were acquired through a nonprofit purchasing collaborative, and supplies and other essential items were purchased through an online wholesale company. All offices in this building were wired for high-speed Internet access. The building owner also subsidized the rent.

❖ ENVIRONMENT

HCI existed in a very rich local environment. Oregon was the first state in the United States to adopt a comprehensive, publicly funded health insurance program for otherwise uninsured people—the Oregon Health Plan. As a result of this environment, a high level of managed care organizations developed, particularly in the tricounty metropolitan region. Although the local community began in 2001 to exhibit characteristics seen in many other local markets where managed care began to dwindle, nonetheless the aftereffects of group practice, limited choice of provider, and employer-supported health insurance as a benefit of employment remained. There was a very active and competitive health insurance market, made up of both local and national companies.

The local health services environment was considered unique in the nation. There was a high degree of collaboration, rather than competition, among the large integrated health systems that were the key members of the Portland Collaborative. These members controlled 90% of inpatient service in the health care market. Their affiliated clinics and medical practices claimed to have approximately 75% of the primary care market share. In 1993, these systems had created the Portland Collaborative as an independent nonprofit entity through which they could collaborate on decision making that in other communities would be highly competitive. Over the years, their projects ranged from coordination of expensive high-technology specialty services, such as cardiac surgery and neonatal intensive care, to working together to establish communitywide immunization programs for children. There was a strong public health presence in each of the three counties in the Portland metropolitan area, and the three county health departments worked together closely through the Tri-County Board of Health and collaborated effectively with the state health department.

The Portland tricounty region had a population of approximately 1.5 million and was a mix of urban and rural communities, including both the highest urban concentration within the state and isolated agricultural communities. The local economy was diverse and had boomed in the past 10 years. Growth sectors included high technology (e.g., computer chips), apparel (e.g., outdoor gear), and agriculture (e.g., wine and microbreweries). The local demographics were changing, with a significant increase in the Latino population. This change was particularly marked in the rural areas where there were large numbers of migrant workers who were essential to the agriculture industry.

Although these environmental conditions presented many opportunities, HCI was also confronted with a serious challenge during 1999 and 2000 because of the increasing competition for grants from both private and public sources. What had been viewed as opportunities suitable only for HCI were being actively pursued by other groups such as the county health departments, local foundations, and other nonprofit organizations, many of which had a much stronger independent resource base than HCI. For example, when the Health Resources and Services Administration, the federal agency responsible for health workforce planning and development, issued a request for proposals for an initiative to support local healthy communities initiatives, HCI attempted to create a local collaborative to submit a joint proposal only to find out that both a local foundation and the tricounty board of health were submitting independent proposals and were unwilling to join a collaborative. This left HCI without a sufficient base from which to build a strong proposal.

In addition, many community groups were participating in new community collaboratives with organizations other than HCI, and these networks were increasingly competitive for funds. Thus, groups such as We Care About Communities, which evolved from a parish nursing program, and the Park Blocks Homeless Youth Coalition, which represented a number of providers of alcohol, drug, housing, and employment training services for youth, were able to create very focused missions and concrete proposals to potential funders in contrast to the often general developmental focus of HCI.

❖ CURRENT CHALLENGES

Four major challenges were now facing the board:

1. Irving Glick, the well-respected community leader who led the Collaborative's advisory committee and then served as the first president of the HCI board, relocated out of the state when his wife took a high-profile health policy position in Washington, DC. Glick had strong community connections across a number of sectors and community groups and facilitated many opportunities for HCI through these connections. This left a recognizable void in the leadership because Glick had been a strong, committed, charismatic, and, at times, controlling board chair. A new president, Beverly Adams, was appointed, but her work commitments with Happy Teeth, a multistate, for-profit chain of dental clinics for which she was the government relations director, prevented her from providing the kind of hands-on leadership that had become standard practice with Glick. Thus some members of the board were concerned about how this less involved board leadership would influence daily HCI operations.

2. The new fiscal year would begin in two months in January 2002. In 2001, HCI had exhausted all carryover funds from existing grants; received 40% less support from the local health systems than in the past as part of the agreement to become an independent organization; secured a small contract to provide services to a county health department; and completed several short-term projects for other community nonprofit organizations. Although HCI had submitted several letters of inquiry

and grant proposals, overall its grant-writing efforts had not been successful. For 2002, HCI had a commitment of continued donations from the health systems for that year only, anticipated continuing to work for at least one of the local county health departments, and hoped to raise significant revenue from grants. However, there was substantial uncertainty among the board members as to whether money would be forthcoming in the short term, and the treasurer had indicated that in six months HCI might no longer be fiscally solvent.

3. Two of HCI's three employees had resigned in the last two months. The program coordinator had accepted a higher-paying job in the private sector, and the administrative assistant had assumed a telemarketing job that she could do from home in order to spend more time with her new baby and save on child care costs. Phyllis Gupta, the executive director, could not do all of the work alone, but the board was reluctant to commit to new staff given fiscal uncertainties of the organization. Gupta had hired a temporary administrative assistant to help in the office and was working with several graduate students to maintain progress on some of the projects. She was eager to hire staff and felt that decisions about staffing as well as organizational directions needed to be made soon.

4. The board was not at its full complement of members. Two new board members had been recruited in the past year, but there were questions among the board as to whether additional board members should be recruited given the uncertainties facing the organization. As well, two members of the board were original members and they were expressing fatigue and suggesting they might resign in order to be replaced by "new blood" who would have more energy and commitment to HCI. Other board members were reluctant to see these two members leave because of the potential loss of organizational memory.

❖ THE BOARD MEETING

As the new fiscal year rapidly approached, the board and the executive director met to decide what to do. The goal of the board meeting was to analyze the strategic and operational issues HCI faced and to develop a list of priority action steps for the board and the director. The agenda for the board meeting was presented (see Appendix 3.3). The summary of expenses and revenues to be presented as part of the agenda was developed (see Appendix 3.4).

Executive Director Gupta gaveled the meeting to order and began, "We need to decide our future."

APPENDIX 3.1

HCI Board of Directors

President: Beverly Adams. Government relations director for a multistate, for-profit chain of dental clinics ("Happy Teeth"). Board member for four years. Very effective in her job but is not a particularly strong board president and does not manage conflict well.

Vice President: Roberto Garcia. Consultant with state and local government public health experience; specialist in migrant health issues. Board member for two years, appointed within one month of his move to the Portland region. Thinks HCI is a good thing but has been marginalized by other board members because of his preoccupation with migrant health issues and unwillingness to recognize that there are multiple valid community health issues that HCI could address.

Secretary: Jacqueline Davis. School health expert for a state government agency; particular interests in teen pregnancy, sexually transmitted diseases, and drug/alcohol abuse. Original board member, and only African American to have served on the Board for longer than one year. Believes HCI should continue to exist regardless of challenges.

Treasurer: Benjamin Wong. High-level social services policy manager of the Tri-County Region Board of Health. HCI Board member for four years. Also Region Board representative to Planning and Operations Committee (POC) of the Portland Collaborative, and currently POC chair. Strong advocate of HCI but has even stronger allegiance to the health board where he works. Despite his visible presence as a leader in the local Asian community, resents being "pigeonholed" as a token advocate for all minorities.

William Evans. Professor of public administration and health at Portlandia University, the urban comprehensive university. Expertise in community development, evaluation, and strategic planning; also facilitator of student placements with HCI. Original board member. Strong supporter of HCI but recognizes that organization is becoming fiscally insolvent and has indicated he would support dissolution if there is no other choice.

Joyce Fargo. Health promotion manager for the Sisters of Mount Hood Health System, a tricounty, Catholic health care provider. New board member. Strong supporter of faith-based activities, and equally strong opponent of any activities that challenge her religious values and beliefs. Lives on a farm in rural Washington County, and to date has been adamant about representing her perceptions of urban versus rural disparities in health services provision in the region.

Angela Gilmore. Retired community activist with university, local government, and faith community ties. New board member. Has a good memory of virtually every community development activity that has either succeeded or failed in the Portland region over the past two decades. Previously a member of the Portland City Council and also served as chair of the local United Way campaign for many years.

George Hume. Nonprofit health care clinic manager. Board member for three years. Has always been skeptical about HCI, feeling that it may be draining community resources that his organization might otherwise be able to access. Active community advocate committed to grassroots organizing on land use and environmental health issues.

Ex officio: Phyllis Gupta. Executive Director, Healthy Communities, Inc. Has held this position for three years. Received a combined MPH/MPA from Portlandia University, where Professor Evans was her mentor, and initially worked at HCI as part of a required field experience. Before that she worked in various nonprofits as a community advocate and organizer and has past working relationships with both Hume and Gilmore.

APPENDIX 3.2

Organizational Membership of the Portland Collaborative*

Hospital and Clinics of the Medical College of Cascadia
Sisters of Mount Hood Health System
Inter-faith Health System
Collaborative Health System and Medical Group, Inc.
Quality Health System
Tri-County Region Board of Health
Tri-State Health Insurance Company
Association of Portland Area Hospitals, Health Systems, and Primary Care Providers

*The governing board of the Portland Collaborative consisted of the Chief Executive Officers of each of these eight organizations, and met quarterly. As well, each CEO designated a senior level executive to be their representative on the Planning and Operations Committee (POC), which met monthly.

APPENDIX 3.3

Healthy Communities Inc. Monthly Board Meeting Agenda

1. Welcome

2. Agree upon detailed agenda for this meeting

3. Staffing

4. Financial report

5. Recruitment of new board members

6. Marketing update

7. Board leadership

8. Decisions on priorities

9. Other business

10. Next meeting

Adjourn

APPENDIX 3.4:

HCI Summary of Expenses and Revenues

	Current Year	Next Year
Beginning balance	$68,000	$48,000
Expenses		
General	7,000	10,000
Personnel/benefits	185,000	165,000
Other program costs	10,000	10,000
Total	$202,000	$185,000
Revenues		
Donations	$60,000	$60,000
Fees and contracts	20,000	30,000
Grants	100,000	53,000
Interest	2,000	2,000
Total	$182,000	$145,000
Ending balance	$48,000	$8,000

❖ NOTES

1.   Although some of the information in this case is real and is derived from the experiences of Healthy Communities of the Columbia-Willamette, Inc., some of the details of the case have been fictionalized. Nothing represented in this case should be interpreted as an accounting of the work of Healthy Communities of the Columbia-Willamette, Inc.; all interpretation is the work of the authors for the purposes of creating a useful teaching case.

2.   See, for example, the Web site of the Coalition of Healthier Cities and Communities at www.healthycommunities.org.

❖ SUGGESTED READINGS

Bielefeld, W. (1994). What affects nonprofit survival? *Nonprofit Management and Leadership, 5*(1), 19–36.

Bryson, J. (1998). *Strategic planning for public and nonprofit organizations.* San Francisco: Jossey-Bass.

Gelmon, S. B., McBride, L., Hill, S., Chester, L., & Guernsey, J. (1999). Portland Tri-County Healthy Communities Initiative: Evaluation Report of the Community Care Network Demonstration, 1996–1998. Portland, OR: Portland State University.

Herman, R. D., & Renz, D. O. (2000). Board practices of especially effective and less effective nonprofit organizations. *American Review of Public Administration, 30*(2), 146–160.

Middleton, M. (1987). Nonprofit boards of directors: Beyond the governance function. In W. W. Powell (Ed.), *The nonprofit sector: A research handbook.* New Haven, CT: Yale University Press.

Mitchell, S. M., & Shortell, S. M. (2000). The governance and management of community health partnerships: A typology for research, policy, and practice. *Milbank Quarterly, 78*(2), 241–281.

Weiner, B. J., & Alexander, J. A. (1998). The challenges of governing public-private community health partnerships. *Health Care Management Review, 23*(2), 39–55.

4

Ending Welfare As We Know It? Cabarrus County Implements Welfare Reform

Gary R. Rassel

❖ BACKGROUND

Cabarrus County had begun its own welfare reform program when the state government started a welfare reform initiative. Shortly thereafter, the federal government enacted welfare reform legislation. Both the state program and the legislative requirements for implementing the national welfare reform program were layered on top of the existing Cabarrus County program. These efforts caused various changes to

AUTHOR'S NOTE: The author wishes to thank the Z. Smith Reynolds Foundation of Winston-Salem, NC, and the University of North Carolina at Chapel Hill for financial assistance and Beth Etringer for research help.

take place in the county government, especially in the Department of Social Services (DSS).

In 1996 President Bill Clinton signed into law the Personal Responsibility and Work Opportunity Reconciliation Act of 1996 (PRWORA) to reform the national welfare system and to "end welfare as we know it." This act abolished the Aid to Families With Dependent Children (AFDC) program and in its place created the Temporary Aid to Needy Families (TANF) block grant program. Along with these changes the legislation was intended to devolve responsibilities from the federal government to state governments. State governments were expected to devolve responsibilities to counties. In order to receive funding from the federal government, each state had to develop plans for moving families off welfare rolls into productive employment. Within each state, county governments were largely responsible for implementing TANF. The federal legislation put a ceiling on funding and a five-year lifetime limit on benefits for any individual. With these restrictions, states not only had to help families move toward self-sufficiency, they had to help ensure that former welfare families and low-income working families had the support they needed to remain self-sufficient.

With TANF, states were given broad flexibility to structure their programs and services to meet national requirements and achieve the four program goals of the legislation. Since the passage of the act, states and localities have used this flexibility to develop and implement a wide range of organizational and program changes. The states were also given increased flexibility to restructure their workforce programs and to craft new approaches to financing child care and medical benefits for low-income families. Combined with a strong economy, these changes produced unprecedented reductions in welfare caseloads and a substantial increase in the number of current and former welfare recipients who were working. Early research indicated that welfare reform worked best where county and state governments had come together early to develop a common agenda; that transportation needs were greater than any other concern; and that placing individuals with multiple barriers to employment in long-term jobs was a growing problem. A downturn in the economy that began in 2000 and continued into 2001 created uncertainty about the continuation of these methods of support. In addition, many former welfare recipients were working in low-wage jobs that might not sustain them and that were most likely to be terminated in a weak economy.

Several states, including California, Wisconsin, and North Carolina, had developed welfare reform programs before the federal government's welfare reform initiative. In 1995, North Carolina Governor James B. Hunt began a welfare reform program called Work First, which had as one of its goals the reduction in welfare rolls through employment of welfare recipients. The rationale was that welfare recipients first needed jobs to provide them with work and a paycheck; training, counseling, and methods for self-reliance would then follow. Governor Hunt began Work First by executive order in July 1995. In July 1996, the federal government granted waivers to the federal welfare program allowing the state to institute work requirements and time limits for support.

In 1997, 1998, and 1999, the conservative, Republican North Carolina General Assembly passed and Governor Hunt, a Democrat, signed various pieces of legislation to modify the state's welfare reform program. As a result, many of the provisions of the governor's Work First program were incorporated into legislation. One legislative provision gave certain local governments significant control over their welfare programs.

Work First was North Carolina's plan to help families move from welfare to jobs and to stay off welfare. It was not just a cash assistance program but was built on the belief that people had responsibilities to families and community to work and provide for children. Work First meant what it said. Work was required for families on welfare to receive assistance. The program was based on the premise that by working, parents could get short-term training and families could get child care and other services to help them become self-sufficient. Most families had two years to move off welfare. At the end of that time, cash assistance ended as did many other modes of support.

Three strategies formed the basis for Work First:

1. Diversion—to keep families off welfare by helping them cope with unexpected emergencies or setbacks. Under Work First, qualifying families could receive up to three months of cash diversion assistance, child care, Food Stamp benefits, and Medicaid, if they stayed off welfare.

2. Work—to shorten the length of time that families were on welfare by making work mandatory and by limiting the length of time families could receive cash assistance. To receive Work First benefits parents had to register with an Employment Assistance Program and sign a mutual responsibility agreement. Once they moved into the phased-in work requirement they could continue to receive benefits for up to 24 months. Families reaching the 24-month limit could not reapply for welfare for three years.

3. Retention—to help families that left welfare to stay off by encouraging them to save and to make sure they really were better off working than on welfare. Work First increased limits on savings and cars, and the state legislature raised income eligibility limits for subsidized child care to ease the burden on low-income, working families. To help clients stay employed, counties also provided retention services such as transportation for families who left the rolls because they got a job.

The state legislation required each county to develop a local Work First block grant plan describing strategies to achieve and measure statewide outcome goals. The plans had to include strategies for reducing county welfare rolls and for placing the former welfare recipients in paying jobs. A variety of groups were allowed the opportunity to provide input to the plans. The General Assembly also required each county to declare itself either a *standard* or an *electing* county. This difference was based on the relationship between North Carolina's DSS and the county government, including the counties' DSS.

The legislation gave the counties' DSS the option of providing a range of services for families with incomes at or below 200% of the federal poverty level as long as they met the eligibility criteria. This was important in helping former welfare families stay off welfare and was also a critical source of services for helping at-risk families who had never been on welfare to stay off welfare.

Under the welfare reform legislation adopted by the North Carolina legislature at the end of the 1997 session, some counties were allowed to determine eligibility and benefits for welfare recipients. Counties could set their own eligibility and benefit standards or continue to operate under the state's eligibility and benefit requirements. Standard counties would operate under the rules of the state DSS; electing counties had more flexibility in setting their rules. Counties were required to submit their Work First plans and decide on either electing or standard status by October 1, 1999.

The number of families on welfare in North Carolina dropped from 113,485 in June 1995 to 47,349 in February 2000. A robust economy and the involvement of numerous nongovernmental organizations contributed to this progress. Businesses, faith communities, and nonprofit organizations were all involved in the effort to move welfare recipients from welfare—receiving cash assistance—to work and self-sufficiency. These nongovernmental organizations aided the effort by hiring Work

First participants; providing transportation to work or training activities; establishing clothing closets; providing classes on job readiness, parenting, and financial planning; and other activities.

In most states, the state rather than local governments administered social services programs. However, in North Carolina counties administered most social services programs under the state's supervision. This system of county-administered, state-supervised social services reflected the state's history of local responsibility for public social services, the strength of county government in the state, and the role of North Carolina's counties as an important mechanism for the delivery of basic services to citizens (Mason, 1999). The major social services programs were based in federal law, funded in part by the federal government, and involved complicated relationships among the federal, state, and county governments.

North Carolina's Department of Health and Human Services (DHHS) was the state executive department responsible for most public human services programs. The governor appointed the secretary of DHHS who in turn appointed the directors of various divisions that issued policies and program manuals for use by county departments of social services. The state DSS oversaw the counties' administration of public assistance programs including Work First. The division provided consultation and technical assistance to counties, developed policies, and conducted training for county staff. With the exception of two large counties, all 100 North Carolina counties had a social services department headed by a director selected by the county social services board. The director, through the social services staff, administered the public assistance and service programs. The department was also the local agency responsible for administering the child support enforcement program in many counties.

Public assistance programs provided financial assistance as direct money payments to recipients, cash-like benefits, and other resources. State law required counties to administer certain public assistance programs that involved a mix of federal, state, and county funding. Counties could provide nonmandated financial assistance programs with county funds (Mason, 1999).

North Carolina implemented the TANF program administratively in October 1996 when the state submitted a plan to the U.S. Department of Health and Human Services to convert the state's AFDC program to a new Work First program for needy families with children. In 1997, the North Carolina General Assembly enacted state welfare reform legislation establishing the Work First program statutorily and making changes to it through subsequent legislation. Major characteristics of this legislation affecting counties included

1. the shift from open-ended to capped, or block grant, funding;

2. an increase in flexibility, especially in the area of services;

3. the ability of a limited number of counties to be "electing" counties, with local authority to set eligibility criteria, payment levels, and other program features;

4. the expanded involvement of other state and local agencies in both planning and implementing programs; and

5. the strong emphasis on, as well as reporting requirements for, measuring program results. (Mason, 1999)

The Work First program was a public assistance and social services program that provided temporary assistance to help needy families with children to become self-sufficient through employment. It consisted of six components: Work First family assistance (time-limited financial assistance); Work First diversion assistance (short-term cash payments to reduce the likelihood of a family's receiving Work First family assistance); Work First services (services designed to help families become self-sufficient); First Stop employment registration; First Stop employment services; and Work First administration (Mason, 1999).

Every two years the state DHHS had to prepare a two-year state Work First plan that included provisions applicable to all counties, provisions applicable to the standard (nonelecting) counties, and approved county plans from the electing counties. The plan had to be approved and submitted to the General Assembly by May 15 of each even-numbered year. Before doing this, DHHS had to seek review from and consult with local governments and private sector organizations, allowing these entities 45 days to comment on the plan.

Both standard and electing counties had to develop biennial Work First plans and submit them to the state DHHS for approval. In standard counties, the county DSS developed the plan and described the Work First diversion assistance and Work First services that the county would provide. The county board of commissioners appointed a committee to identify the needs of the population to be served and to assist the county DSS in developing the plan. By January 15 of each even-numbered year, the board of commissioners had to approve the county Work First plan and submit it to DHHS for approval.

In electing counties, the Board of County Commissioners developed the county's Work First plan but also appointed a committee to identify the needs of the population to be served and to assist in developing the plan. The plan had to describe conditions in the county, outcomes and goals, how the Work First program would be administered, and funding requirements. An electing county's plan also had to describe county policies relating to benefit level, eligibility for assistance asset and income requirements, time limits and extensions, and sanctions.

❖ THE COUNTY

Cabarrus County, North Carolina, was located in the Charlotte-Gastonia-Rock Hill Metropolitan Statistical Area in the southwest central part of the state. In 1990, its population was 98,935. By 2000, it had grown to 131,063, a 32.5% increase. By comparison, the population of North Carolina had increased by 21.4% over the same time. In 1999, 53.8% of the residents (65,610 people) were in the workforce. In 1990, 67% of county residents had a high school degree and 12.3% had a college degree. About 73% of high school graduates went on to college, a figure somewhat below the state average. The high school dropout rate from 1998 to 1999 was 3.8%. Between 1995 and early spring of 2000, the unemployment rate dropped from 3.5 to 2.0%. In 1999, per capita income was about $24,000, exceeding the state average. However, in 1995, 28% of employed county residents earned less than the poverty level, and in 1998, 4% of the population (about 4,780 persons) were on Food Stamps. Between July 1997 and June 1999, the number of families eligible for Work First declined from 594 to 407, a decrease of 31.5%. These families were those eligible for financial support for a limited time while working or looking for employment.

In 1999, the four largest employment sectors in the county and the percentage of the workforce employed in each were manufacturing, 26.8%; government, 18.1%; retail trade, 17.6%; and services, 17.3%. The North Carolina Department of Commerce rated Cabarrus County as one of the five least economically distressed counties in the state. Although the majority of residents were Caucasian and the largest minority group was African American, the number of Hispanic and

Asian Americans had increased rapidly after 1995. The increased presence of minorities was obvious in the large number of stores with signs in Spanish and Vietnamese as well as the increased numbers of these groups among the clients of many public agencies. These agencies partially adjusted to the largest area of increased population by providing Spanish lessons for employees. According to the 2000 census, the minority population in the county was 15.7%, having increased from 13.3% in 1999.

The Cabarrus County DSS was governed by an appointed five-member County Board of Social Services. This board provided direction to the department and evaluated the director's performance. The social services board in turn reported to the Board of County Commissioners. Two of the five board members were appointed by the state, the county commissioners appointed another two, and these four elected the fifth board member. The social services board was the hiring authority for the director of social services, advised the director on agency operations including developing the budget, and provided community and social planning. The board was also a conduit for communicating with the elected County Board of Commissioners, which had the authority to approve the county social services budget. The State DHHS provided statewide policy for the administration of programs but did not have personnel authority at the local level.

The Political Context

Cabarrus County was governed by a five-member Board of County Commissioners who served four-year terms. Commissioners were elected on a staggered basis every two years; three seats were filled during one election, and two were filled during the following election.

Republicans had dominated electoral politics in the county during the 1990s. In 1998, 65% of Cabarrus County residents (78,266) were registered to vote. Of those registered, 43% were Democrats, 42% were Republicans, and 16% were unaffiliated. Despite an almost equal number of registered Republicans and Democrats in the county, the commissioners were all Republican. In fact, Republicans had held every seat on the board since 1990. According to one commissioner, "Cabarrus is a conservative county with a conservative governing board, but a board willing to think outside of the box." This commissioner noted that some members of the board were not originally from the county and had been important in introducing and implementing new ideas. She did add, however, that with the fall 2000 elections the board "might be moving in a direction that was too conservative." This comment was prompted in part by the fact that two conservative Republican candidates defeated two moderate incumbent Republican members of the board of commissioners in a primary election earlier in the year.

In recent years, the board had also seen more women candidates for commissioner. In the 1996 election, three women—two Republicans and one Democrat—competed for two seats on the board. The Republicans, Carolyn Carpenter and Sue Casper, won and were two of only four women to have served on the board. Casper was the chair of the board of commissioners when the Work First plan was approved.

Managing growth and tax increases were important issues in the county commissioners race in 1998. Two of three commissioners elected in that year belonged to the Cabarrus Taxpayers Association (CTA), which opposed a 1-cent sales tax and 1% real estate transfer tax. "I think that the results show people like the job [the current commission chair] has done and that our message of no new taxes has gotten through," said one of the newly elected commissioners.

Time Frame—Highlights

Cabarrus County had attempted to provide alternatives to welfare for several years. A JOBS program was started in 1988. An education and training program targeting young mothers, JOBS provided assistance to recipients while they were in school. In 1995, the director of the county DSS, James Cook, proposed a "workfare" program that would use a grant diversion of AFDC and Food Stamps money for a portion of an hourly wage to be paid to the recipient. Thus, the cash would be used to supplement the income of welfare recipients. "What we want to do is turn the welfare program into a work opportunity program," Cook said. Fletcher Hartsell, then chair of the social services board, and members of the Board of County Commissioners were supportive. They were interested in improving the old system because it did not produce the results they wanted. There were not sufficient financial incentives nor disincentives for staying off welfare. The chair of the board of commissioners, Jeff Barnhart, said, "Somehow we have got to break that cycle [of welfare] and this is a way to do it." Commissioners and DSS employees were aware of workfare programs under way in California, Wisconsin, and other states and thought it worthwhile to attempt something similar in Cabarrus County.

Approval to implement the workfare program required state legislation. Hartsell, who was also a state senator, sponsored Cook's ideas through legislation in the General Assembly. Cook, members of his staff, the Board of County Commissioners, Hartsell, and other members of the General Assembly from Cabarrus County worked hard to get the legislation passed. They lobbied legislative committees in Raleigh, the state capitol. In June 1995, the state legislature authorized Cabarrus County to establish an AFDC and Food Stamp pilot program and an adjunct demonstration program modifying the JOBS program. That legislation made Cabarrus the only county in the state with legislative approval for welfare reform. This allowed the county to establish a program called Work Over Welfare (WOW). The DSS cited WOW as being largely responsible for the 40% decrease in caseload that the county experienced between the time WOW was created in 1995 and when the Work First plan was established in 1997.

The DSS director and other employees of the department were instrumental in designing the WOW program. In addition to changing the focus of welfare, the department underwent other structural and pro-cedural changes to improve how it did business. These included chang-ing the nature of the job of the social services workers from determining eligibility to being employment counselors. Some county service sites were relocated and the way work was done was reorganized. The county expanded its working relationships with businesses and nonprofit organizations. The North Carolina Association of County Directors of Social Services in 1995 named Cook DSS Director of the Year. The associ-ation's president said that Cook "embodies the best in creativity, tenacity, fiscal responsibility and ability to navigate the morass of people who have said 'we can't do that' " ("*Cook Named DSS Director of the Year,*" 1995).

Decision Dynamics

In October 1997, Cabarrus County officials decided to develop a Work First plan for the county under the new electing county status. However, the county could still decide to opt out of this status. The DSS director was concerned over just what becoming an electing county would mean. "We're trying to figure out how much latitude the state is going to give the pilot programs," he said. "We feel like there are some things the state won't let you do."

The Cabarrus Welfare Reform Planning Committee was formed in 1997. Committee members included individuals representing a wide range of government, business, and nonprofit organizations from educational institutions to churches. Cook was facilitator for the committee and his staff assisted its members. The committee had five goals. These were to

1. assess the needs of families,

2. secure public comment,

3. determine how agencies and organizations could work together to provide services and resources,

4. recommend to the board of commissioners a plan that would assist the county in reaching the state's goals, and

5. contribute to the community's implementation and carrying out of the welfare reform plan.

The public was made aware of the planning process through televised board of commissioners' meetings and through newspaper coverage of the planning process. Copies of the plan were located in various places around the county including branches of the library, the Cabarrus County Government Center, and in town halls.

One of the most important factors in the county's plan was a pay for performance concept. Pay for performance meant that in order to receive cash assistance, a person had to work a required number of hours. If the client did not meet those hours, then he or she would not receive cash assistance for that month. DSS Director Cook stated that Cabarrus County "threatened to be *electing* so that they could get pay for performance." The director noted that the state DSS did not really want or like electing county status, but that the state was supportive of pay for performance. He said that "*standard* [status] was good for the state, so was innovation." The county plan was approved for the county to become an electing county but the DSS Director decided to go standard and convinced the board of commissioners to approve his recommendation. The Work First supervisor, Fran O'Conner, described Cabarrus County as "standard with waivers." Pay for Performance was approved and became a part of the county's WOW program.

❖ GOALS, OBJECTIVES, AND PROGRAM PRIORITIES

The Work First plan for Cabarrus County described the means by which the county planned to meet the goals given to them by the state. These goals included the following:

1. Reducing the Work First (welfare) caseload—15%.

2. Putting adults to work—174 adults.

3. Staying off welfare after going to work—85%.

4. Meeting "all parent" participation rate—35%.

5. Meeting "two parent" participation rate—90%.

6. Avoiding welfare through diversion assistance—6%.

7. Increasing child support orders and collections for Work First—10%.

8. Improving child well-being (percentage of Work First children with intensive child protective services with a safety plan)—100%.

The plan called for using several procedures to meet the goal of reducing the Work First caseload. The first procedure was to identify the barriers and factors creating a need for assistance and to remove them. The plan cited lack of child care resources and lack of public transportation as major barriers to job placement for many Work First families.

Diversion assistance and the pursuit of child support payments were viewed as means to help families before they were placed on welfare. *Grant diversion*, where the amount of the cash benefit and Food Stamps was diverted to an employer to be matched for a salary, was part of the plan to put adults to work. County Work First supervisor O'Conner said that diversion assistance was good for many clients because it enabled them to "see light at the end of the tunnel." She also thought that diversion assistance could not have happened before cash assistance was removed as an entitlement. If clients did go on assistance, the county had several ways to try to get them off as soon as possible by assisting them with finding work and becoming self-sufficient.

The DSS worked with the Economic Security Commission (ESC) on a program to help locate jobs. The ESC was the primary deliverer of job placement services in the Work First program. Clients had to register for work with the ESC before the Work First application was processed. To enhance the employability of clients, transportation and child care assistance were available when the client was interviewing, job hunting, or doing other employment-related activities. In addition, the clients were offered formal classes where they learned ways to improve their chances of obtaining and keeping a job.

The Work First plan noted the importance of the WOW program in meeting the goal of putting adults to work. It noted that the county's 40% reduction in caseload between 1995 and 1997 was the result of moving the most employable recipients into jobs; it left a welfare population that was more difficult to assist in finding work. Thus the plan called for simplifying Work First eligibility rules so that the caseworkers could spend more time helping clients find jobs and less time reviewing rules to determine if clients were eligible for assistance. Job-readiness and work experience classes were provided to help those with no work experience or with bad work habits.

Good follow-up and support was emphasized to ensure that clients were stabilized in their jobs before a crisis occurred causing them to quit. The plan called for retaining the case for an unspecified amount of time so that the DSS worker could keep track of the family. It also noted that "WOW incentives, after employment, will make it possible for clients to afford to stay off welfare and remain working." The most important means to help the client keep working, according to the plan, was checking with the employee and employer periodically and urging clients to call a DSS worker if they felt that they could not handle a situation or if a crisis situation occurred. The Work First plan noted that the lack of reliable transportation was a common reason that clients lost jobs and called for funding from the state Department of Transportation to help solve this problem.

DSS employees used several strategies to reduce state and local expenditures. These included diversion assistance where a check, worth up to three months of Work First benefits, could be given to the client. Money from the emergency assistance fund could also be given to the family instead of automatically placing them on the welfare rolls. The chair of the board of social services reported that the county and DSS had not saved money, but that money was used differently and more effectively. Money was no longer being given out as cash assistance. After welfare reform, money was used to provide vehicles for recipients, to help them pay for day care, and in a variety of other ways. Money was given to clients to aid them to get on their feet and to establish themselves in their jobs. According to O'Conner, reducing state and local expenditures was not really a major concern—the concern was with getting people to work so they could support themselves.

The Work First plan stated that "Cabarrus County will take any steps necessary to protect children." It called for increasing child support orders and collections for Work First children. These steps helped reduce a family's need for public assistance and the county's expenditures. The steps also helped to ensure that children were being supported by the absent parent. Any child in the Child Welfare system whose family was on Work First had a safety plan. Social workers from both agencies coordinated services for the family and the child. After a Work First family left welfare, or if a family was not receiving benefits because they were not performing their work responsibilities, the family's case was still followed by a DSS employee for a month. Social workers followed families in other situations to ensure the welfare of the children.

Wayne Trexler, the chair of the board of social services, noted that the main goal of WOW and Work First was to get people to be self-supporting and self-sufficient and to not be dependent on the government. When Trexler was asked by a state DSS worker what the main goal of WOW was, he responded, "to put you out of work, and to dissolve DSS."

❖ PROGRAM IMPLEMENTATION

Before welfare reform, according to some employees, DSS workers only identified those eligible for welfare and made certain that they received benefits. DSS workers would ask, "What are you applying for?" and, if the clients were eligible, would help them obtain the cash or other assistance to which they were entitled. That approach changed with reform. Now DSS workers ask, "I understand that you are having problems, what do you need help with?" Work First Supervisor O'Conner said that the emphasis changed from the DSS workers quickly getting the family onto the welfare roll and providing cash benefits to DSS workers figuring out how to help families get out of the situations they were in.

Use of Funds

Frank Clifton, the county manager, and Commissioner Carpenter also noted that the money given to DSS was spent in a different way after welfare reform. It was used to provide transportation and day care so that these common barriers to work could be overcome. Some money was also used to help clients overcome substance abuse problems. Trexler noted that the county commissioners had been willing to spend money for DSS because they felt that DSS had been reasonable in managing money allocated to them. He thought that if changes in DSS operations had not occurred, DSS and the board of commissioners probably would have fought over the budget. State waivers of regulations that enabled department employees to do a better job were also thought to be important. The DSS director said that the state was benefiting from not having to give as much money for welfare but the county was not really gaining additional revenue.

Organizational and Cultural Changes

The county had implemented many changes in organization and procedure at the same time welfare reform was implemented. The DSS, the Health Department, and the Mental Health Department were relocated from separate buildings into the same, newly renovated building in 1998. This relocation made county services more accessible. Because many residents seeking social services were also in need of health and mental health services, this merger improved the one-stop shopping aspect of county services.

The county was also the first in the state to use a single-application process whereby clients could apply for many types of services without filling out a multitude of applications and having to make several trips to the DSS office. This new process reduced paperwork and gave more time to the employees to help families. The board of commissioners saw it as a way to save money. Today, almost every county in the state uses this application process.

DSS changed the approach to eligibility determination, case review, and case management. The goal of service was changed and more services were provided by teams of employees rather than a single caseworker. DSS Director Cook called the new process a "Reengineering of the Corporation." The role of many employees changed. According to the director, this role change was hard for them. He said many had made a career out of being welfare eligibility experts, and they were "real comfortable" in that role. However, "reform changed that."

In the past a DSS employee could look at an applicant's dollar figures (the person's income, the value of the family car, the value of the home) and determine whether or not the family would be eligible for welfare services. After welfare reform, decisions were not as clear-cut. According to the director, for many employees, welfare reform had become a "pain in the neck." There was more confusion, more work, and more complexity for the DSS workers. As they gained more experience with Work First, however, the grumbling decreased as "employees realized that this was how it was going to be."

Range of Players

Cabarrus County employed both public and private resources to aid their Work First families. Among the public agencies were the Employment Security Commission, Vocational Rehabilitation, and Mental Health Departments. The county also had a relationship with the community college to help provide training, the public schools to help those on welfare and in school to graduate, and the housing authority.

Commissioner Carpenter thought the private and nonprofit sectors were used more in aiding welfare clients than before welfare reform. She cited a recent change in which more private doctors were involved in treating welfare recipients. Others noted that DSS seemed to work more closely with some private-sector organizations by contracting out and engaging on-site workers. O'Conner pointed out that although the economy was in good shape and welfare recipients had several opportunities, some stores regularly hired welfare participants. The chamber of commerce was also an important liaison between DSS/Work First and the businesses.

Churches provided valuable aid to welfare families including supportive services, such as transportation and child care. Members helped to serve as mentors and instill a work ethic. Some church congregations were asked to adopt individuals on a one-on-one basis to provide specific needs. Cooperative Christian Ministries and the Salvation Army were beneficial in helping families in crisis situations. County Manager Clifton said that churches and other nonprofit agencies had found a bigger niche in which to be involved following welfare reform.

Those involved seemed to feel that welfare reform had achieved some success in Cabarrus County, although different actors had differing opinions about the amount of success and the durability of any changes. Most attributed the changes to the actions of local officials and employees, however, rather than to the state-level Work First initiatives. DSS Director Cook, State Senator Hartsell, DSS employees, and members of the county commission and board of social services all contributed in their own ways to changes in the provision of welfare services in the county.

County and State Relations

Commissioner Carpenter noted that Cabarrus County was well represented in the state legislature. That in turn helped the county's relationship with state agencies. Hartsell was an important factor in designing changes in the welfare reform process in Cabarrus County as well as in representing the county's initiatives and requests to the state legislature. Because of him, the state gave the county more leeway to try new things. Commissioner Carpenter said that reform helped to "open the arena for innovation." Cook agreed with this assessment. He said that DSS had more flexibility now than before welfare reform. There may be more rules, Cook said, but there were also more options. However, at times the relationship between county officials and state DSS officials was strained. By 2000 the relationship between county and state DSS was more cooperative than in the past and as a result the county had more flexibility and autonomy.

Successes, Achievements, and Positive Results

The biggest success resulting from welfare reform in Cabarrus County may have been the change in outlook of the recipients and the impact of this on their lives. Work First Supervisor O'Conner said that the reform helped to put people to work in stable jobs and helped them to provide for their children. She said that it changed the recipient's outlook on life in a positive way. The social services board chair said that the reform made people self-supporting. Welfare recipients were able to see that they could leave welfare and provide for their families. Commissioner Carpenter said that welfare recipients had "self-esteem that they didn't have before." She and others made it clear that welfare reform had provided more than just a job or just a handout. It was truly making a difference in the lives of people. Carpenter thought that reform had broken the welfare cycle.

O'Conner was pleased with retention—the number of people who did not return to the welfare rolls. She said that the decrease was possible because of the day care and transportation support that the county helped obtain for those who had a job and wanted to work. Cabarrus County had no public transportation system, and many new workers could not find affordable day care. According to Carpenter, the county was able to do all of this and still have a reasonable budget—pleasing both county commissioners and residents.

DSS Director Cook said that families received more help after welfare reform; however, it was not simply a result of reform that caused this. He said DSS had "improved what we are all about." The county was willing to invest resources in providing services to individuals who would work and keep working. As long as there seemed to be an end to providing services, and if the services were not in the form of cash gifts to those who could but chose not to work, this very politically conservative county seemed willing to provide the resources.

Shortcomings, Barriers, Problems, and Failures

Along with all the successes of welfare reform there were also failures. O'Conner was upset because, with the emphasis on Work First, people were not able to take advantage of educational programs as they had under the JOBS program. She called it a "missed opportunity" for people to go to school. With the time limit on benefits, many clients who could have benefited from technical training programs were not able to do so. The current board of social services chair, Trexler, said that there would always be some failures—"not everyone would get off the rolls." An opinion voiced by many employees and elected officials was that welfare had not really been reformed, but rather that some changes were made and that much of the success could be attributed to a robust economy. Trexler even noted that if the economy turned sour for a long period the county might be back to the old ways again. However, he thought that the changes taking place from 1995 to 2000 had been beneficial.

County Manager Clifton and Commissioner Carpenter expressed concern that welfare reform had done little to affect the state of secondary education in the county. They were concerned about the number of students reading below grade level and those who failed to complete high school. Clifton was also concerned about changes taking place in the mental health system. Under a new proposal, the state would require the county to spend a great deal more money on providing services for mental health than before. Although he saw benefits of welfare reform, Clifton saw no short-term savings in county expenditures. He did agree, however, that although welfare had not really been reformed, many important changes had taken place.

❖ ASSESSMENT

In general, elected officials, employees, and board members seemed pleased with the changes in the welfare system in Cabarrus County and with the results. Clearly, however, the process by which these changes were set in motion began well before Work First or TANF was implemented. DSS Director Cook, with the involvement of staff, county commissioners, and social services board members, designed and implemented an innovative approach to providing welfare services, WOW, in 1995. This was before Work First, the state program, was developed and before TANF was implemented, requiring extensive negotiations with state bureaucrats and lobbying of elected officials to obtain necessary waivers.

Work First seemed to mesh well with the WOW program. The state DSS made important changes affecting the culture of the organization and the outlook of its employees before Work First. Although implementing these changes was not easy, they seemed to remain in place. One objective of welfare reform was to change the relationship between state and local government. Devolution—pushing decisions and innovations from the state to the local level—was a term heard often in discussions of welfare reform. Although county-to-state relations had not changed very much, county department employees appeared to have more autonomy from the state and more flexibility to innovate. Employees believed that they had permission to try new approaches on their own. Having realized a certain amount of success with WOW and then with Work First, career and elected officials appeared eager to strike out on their own in other areas without state interference.

One of the components of the TANF legislation was that cash assistance to any individual or family was time-limited. It was no longer an entitlement. At first, many welfare recipients did not accept the fact that benefits would end at a definite time. However, this message seemed to have been quickly driven home and those receiving benefits under TANF understood that they would end. The economy in Cabarrus County between 1996 and 2000 was so robust that the unemployment rate was very low. County officials expressed the belief that any able-bodied person who wanted a job could have one. However, County Manager Clifton, Commissioner Carpenter, and DSS Director Cook were all concerned about what would happen to those recently removed from the welfare rolls if the economy faltered.

By most indicators, Cabarrus County was politically conservative. Hence it was surprising that commissioners were willing to continue to invest resources in welfare. However, they continued to do so only as long as it appeared that these expenditures would result in putting people to work and were not cash entitlements. The attitudes of those involved in the welfare system—including county employees, elected officials, recipients, private nonprofit organizations, and businesses working with the county to provide jobs and services—all seemed to have changed. However, it did not appear that the general public knew much about the changes that had taken place or how they affected policy or administration.

In 2000 Cabarrus County had to revise its Work First plan. This process was not expected to generate much conflict or controversy, as the general impression was that Work First and WOW had been successful. However, the makeup of the board of commissioners changed with two very conservative members replacing two experienced, moderate members. Other stresses affected county government. County expenditures for welfare did not decrease. Changes made in the mental health system by state government promised to increase county financial obligations in this area.

❖ EPILOGUE

In 2000 the U.S. economy started to decline, driven largely, but not only, by losses in the technology sectors. This trend continued to worsen in 2001. The economy of North Carolina was greatly affected by this downturn. Unemployment rates rose as many workers were laid off. For example, between May 2000 and May 2001, the unemployment rate of the Charlotte-Gastonia-Rock Hill Metropolitan Statistical Area, in which Cabarrus County was located, rose from 3.0 to 5.3% of the workforce. The unemployment rate in Cabarrus reached a 16-year high in the spring of 2001. As the stock market suffered, the paper wealth of many people fell significantly. State and local government revenues suffered as tax revenues fell. The downturn in the economy and other factors reduced the revenues available for the North Carolina state budget for fiscal years 2001 and 2002. This in turn affected local governments.

North Carolina approached the end of its 2000–2001 fiscal year with a budget shortfall of nearly $850 million. The state had either to reduce spending or increase revenues or use some combination of these activities to balance the 2000–2001 fiscal year budget while developing the following year's budget. This shortfall resulted from the slowing economy, court decisions requiring North Carolina to return tax money collected in previous years, and the continuing costs of repairing flood damage caused by Hurricane Floyd in 1999.

Since 1990, state government in North Carolina had reimbursed cities and counties for tax revenues no longer available to local governments because of changes in state laws. These reimbursements were an important component of the revenues for local governments. Because of the state budget shortfall, the governor in late 2000 decided to withhold these reimbursements. This happened when local governments were preparing their fiscal year 2001–2002 budgets.

Cabarrus County now faced a faltering economy, a scenario that County Manager Clifton, Commissioner Carpenter, and DSS Director Cook had worried might affect the success of their Work First program. At the same time, the county commissioners had to oversee the preparation of a new Work First plan. The welfare reform act of 1996 was also scheduled for legislative review and reauthorization by Congress in 2002. Congress was scheduled to hold sessions to hear from federal, state, and local administrators and elected officials about how the welfare reform effort worked in the first five years. The results of the first five years and current conditions were sure to affect how Congress viewed reauthorization of PRWORA.

As DSS director, how do you prepare to meet the anticipated impact of economic trends?

❖ REFERENCES

Cook named DSS director of the year. (1995, May 15). *Concord Tribune*, p. A7.

Mason, J. (1999). Social services. In A. F. Bell II & W. J. Wicker (Eds.), *County Government in North Carolina* (4th ed., pp. 693–740). Chapel Hill: North Carolina Institute of Government.

5

Evolving Objectives

*The Statewide Evaluation and
Planning Services Program*

Patricia M. Alt

❖ BACKGROUND

In her fall 2001 graduate public health administration class, the coordinator for aging policy in the Maryland Department of Health and Mental Hygiene (DHMH) gave a brief presentation on her preliminary analysis of the first decade's information from Maryland's Statewide Evaluation and Planning Services (STEPS) assessment process. Since 1987, county health department workers had been doing STEPS assessments on potentially nursing-home-eligible older citizens seeking advice about care options. Even though she had coordinated the interagency committee that produced the STEPS process, the results the coordinator identified from the 1988 to 1997 summary data were puzzling to her.

Although she had hoped to use the data to examine changes in "unmet need" over time, the data showed distinct variations from county to county across the state in assessed levels of disability and in services recommended for plans of care. They also indicated a sharp statewide shift after 1995 in willingness to definitely predict nursing home eligibility. Even for clients who seemed to have similar levels of disability and medical conditions, the suggested care plans were wildly different. Comparing statewide data with that from four adjacent jurisdictions whose populations ranged from urban to rural, she showed the class graphic illustrations of the variety to be found in STEPS results. There were definite shifts in reported levels of eligibility for nursing home care and in disability, in reasons for being referred for an evaluation, and in proposed plans of care (see Appendix 5.1).

The coordinator asked her graduate students, many of whom were employed in local public health programs, to consider what might have been occurring during the period covered by the graphs, and to discuss the potential policy uses of these data. Was the committee that originally designed the STEPS process naive in believing that it would produce information on "unmet need," which could help shape further policy? As workers with direct client contact, what would have shaped their use of the assessment form and what they reported on it? How could they explain the results she was finding?

Slowly, students offered the following suggestions, which were written by the coordinator on a flip chart for further consideration:

1. There might be tremendous differences in type and number of long-term care services available in different counties.

2. Most likely, client income and insurance eligibility varied (including Medicaid) in the counties.

3. Reluctance to give a client a suggested plan of care that cannot be carried out.

4. Ethical concerns about proper practice of their professions.

5. Longitudinal changes within each county are not shown in summary data and statewide data do not show county variations.

6. Changes in the coding options available on the form itself over time affecting the results.

7. Perhaps forms were not submitted for people whose evaluations would not be Medicaid reimbursable, although they were still given care planning help.

8. Local context—in some counties, senior care is much more established and likely to request more frequent reassessments of clients.

9. Differences in what types of clients received STEPS evaluation, based on sources of referral, the local health department's activism in publicizing the program, and the availability of assessments through large hospitals such as the University of Maryland Medical Center and Johns Hopkins Hospital.

10. Needing to recommend the least costly services, in order for the client to afford them, or for their insurance to cover them, recognizing that many home- and community-based services were not covered by insurance.

11. With strong demand for STEPS evaluations, workers might feel pressured to complete them more rapidly than they would under optimal circumstances.

12. Care recommendations depend heavily on what services the client was already using before being evaluated, and the form did not give that information except for those who were already in a nursing home.

13. Although it might help state planners to know about needs that were not being met, frontline workers focus on obtaining immediately useful information.

14. Perhaps repeated careful training sessions by the state DHMH staff had made the evaluations more sophisticated and detailed over time.

After this brainstorming exercise, the students were assigned to four groups (to represent the four counties selected for the project) to discuss the relative importance of each of the points. The counties used were all from the Baltimore Metropolitan Statistical Area (see Table 5.1). They included Baltimore City and Baltimore County, each of which had over-65-year-old populations numbering around 100,000 and whose seniors had constituted more than 13% of their populations

Table 5.1   Comparison of Four Baltimore-Area Jurisdictions

Name of Jurisdiction	Baltimore City	Baltimore County (not including Baltimore City)	Harford County	Cecil County
Type of Jurisdiction	Urban	Inner-Ring Suburb	Outer-Ring Suburb	Rural
Population, 1990	736,014	691,134	182,132	71,347
Population, 2000	651,154	754,292	218,590	85,951
Over 65 Population/ Percentage, 1990	100,916/ 13.7%	96,849/ 13.9%	15,034/ 8.2%	7,365/ 10.3%
Over 65 Population/ Percentage, 2000	85,921/ 13.2%	110,335/ 14.6%	22,160/ 10.1%	8,995/ 10.5%
Number of Nursing Homes, 2000	40	43	4	3
Ratio of Nursing Homes to Over 65 Population, 2000	1:2,148	1:2,566	1:5,540	1:2,998

during the entire period under study. Baltimore City was increasingly poor and losing population. Baltimore County, as an inner-ring suburb (completely surrounding but politically separate from the city), was beginning to deal with some urban issues, while it continued to be the jurisdiction with the largest proportion of its population elderly. The other two counties included were Harford and Cecil. Harford County was at the next level out of suburban development from Baltimore County. Although still much smaller than Baltimore County, Harford saw its population expand rapidly during the 1990s, including its proportion of elderly residents, which was more than 10% by 2000. Cecil County, further north, was even smaller and relatively rural. Its population had aged in place and was also approximately 10% elderly by 2000.

❖   MARYLAND'S PROUD HISTORY OF HEALTH REFORM

Maryland has a long history of innovative public policy efforts in health care. In the 1960s and 1970s, programs were created to reduce length of medical hospital stays or deflect inappropriate psychiatric hospital admissions. In the late 1970s, the focus shifted to ensuring that potential nursing facility patients had maximum opportunity to remain in the community and that nursing facilities would receive adequate compensation from Medical Assistance (also known as Medicaid), to encourage them to admit heavier-care patients, particularly those currently in hospital settings. Medicaid, as the federal-state program covering the majority of care for nursing facility residents, was struggling to get patients out of more costly and less appropriate hospital settings and into nursing facilities or community-based care. Although an increasing proportion of Medicaid's funds was going to nursing facilities, it was technically a program aimed at care for the poor. Older and disabled residents entered nursing facilities with Medicare or private-pay coverage, but once their coverage and their own funds were exhausted, they became financially eligible for Medicaid (usually within a year at the most).

Thus, new programs were created in response to legal pressure and public demand for less restrictive environments. The programs also were strongly influenced by the legislature's desire to save money, to gain accurate information on unmet needs, and to seek federal financial support wherever possible. In 1999, the Adult Evaluation and Review Services (AERS) program in the state and local health departments emerged from the combination and outgrowth of multiple efforts to assist aged and functionally disabled adults who were at risk of institutionalization. Until 1999, the program was known as Geriatric Evaluation Services (GES), despite the fact that it had grown to incorporate several different evaluation services. The program's new name attempted to revise its image to better indicate the array of services it provided, including GES, STEPS, and Preadmission Screening and Resident Reviews (PASRR). Completed by members of the same local health department staff, these evaluations differed in their histories, payment mechanisms, and clients served. All sought to provide information and referral to the most appropriate levels of care for the particular person.

❖ SEEKING COORDINATION
   AMONG OVERLAPPING PROGRAMS

Geriatric Evaluation Services

Stemming originally from the deinstitutionalization movement in mental health care and its focus on appropriate care for the mentally disabled, the GES program provided evaluations by local health department teams of nurses, social workers, and psychologists or psychiatrists to determine whether older patients belonged in nursing facilities, mental hospitals, or other care arrangements. Maryland began the program in Baltimore City in 1969 and mandated it on a statewide basis in 1976. At the time, it was common to seek care in state psychiatric hospitals for community-dwelling older citizens who began to exhibit dementia, for example, and who might be more appropriately (and less expensively) cared for in a nursing home or other setting. In a nursing facility, these patients cost the state less than in a public mental hospital because they could have private-pay coverage or have federal matching funds if on Medicaid. GES always provided a range of medical and psychological evaluations to any citizen over 60, but it was legally required to evaluate any adult 65 years of age or older for whom psychiatric institutionalization was sought. Until the advent of STEPS, GES was entirely supported by state Preventive Medicine Administration (state-only funds) and Medicaid (federal/state funds) grants to local health departments, occasionally supplemented by local budgets. GES teams were fiercely loyal to the vision of fully serving all the elderly citizens of Maryland who asked for evaluations, regardless of financial circumstances. However, although their heavy reliance on state funding preserved their focus on caring for all citizens without regard for financial eligibility, it left GES more vulnerable to legislative cost-cutting pressure.

Community Placement Program

In 1979, Maryland Medicaid began a demonstration Community Placement Program (CPP) to examine the value of providing information, referral, and evaluation services in preventing inappropriate nursing home institutionalization. It was a successor to the predischarge planning program through which Medicaid had sought to facilitate hospital discharges to nursing facilities or community services. Operating in only four jurisdictions—Baltimore City, Baltimore County, Caroline County, and Dorchester County—it paid for local health department staff to evaluate and case manage both current Medicaid patients and those who were considered "potentially" eligible (defined by $750 or less/month income). Each evaluation was paid for by Medicaid with federal financial participation, but it became apparent in the 1980s that the program needed to become statewide in order to maintain the federal matching funds. Although CPP and GES overlapped, their basic premises were different. CPP focused on decreasing nursing home use among current Medicaid clients whatever their age, while GES focused on defining the optimal care plan for an elderly client (often recommending nursing facility admission instead of psychiatric hospitalization) without regard to their Medicaid status.

Gateway II/Senior Care

Beginning in 1983, local interagency advisory committees were set up in nine Maryland counties to coordinate evaluations, case management, and services being provided for frail elderly patients through local health, aging, and social services departments. The primary goal of this "Gateway II" program was to enable people who would otherwise be Medicaid patients in nursing facilities to remain at home as long as possible. The county-level Gateway II demonstrations used "gap-filling" funds from the state budget to purchase needed services that would not otherwise be available. The evaluations were done by local health department GES or CPP staff in the nine counties. However, in most counties, the "lead" agency was the local aging agency. Almost immediately problems arose with the state gap-filling funds being used by the lead agency to finance in-home services and evaluations that could have been funded under federally funded programs (frequently those available through the health or social services departments). Often, the reason given for spending the gap-filling funds was difficulty in getting clients rapidly assessed and admitted into needed service programs found in the other local departments.

In 1984, the Maryland Department of Budget and Fiscal Planning (DBFP) produced a report evaluating four in-home services programs, including Gateway II, and recommended that these programs be more fully funded in order that services be available to those who needed them. However, DBFP also strongly recommended that better procedures be in place to ensure that clients who were eligible for Medicaid received Medicaid-funded services, rather than services reimbursed from state-only funds. In discussing those "at risk" of institutionalization, the DBFP report pointed out the underlying assumption that increasing community-based services would reduce the need for institutionalization. The report stated that "the available data from these and other community programs is not conclusive as to the impact that community programs actually have on institutionalization rates. The effectiveness of community programs in reducing rates of institutionalization would appear to be dependent on the ability to target services, not only to the eligible needy but, more important, to those eligible needy who would actually have been users of institutional care in the absence of community alternatives" (Maryland Department of Budget and Fiscal Planning, 1984). In response, the Office on Aging commissioned its own consultant, Donald Simpson, to produce an evaluation focused on Gateway II and long-term care in Maryland. In January 1986, Simpson recommended integrating Gateway II intake, assessment, and case management in local aging agencies, taking services away from GES/local health departments and from local social service agencies (Simpson, 1986).

Thus, although the state was operating under a legislative mandate to expand the Gateway II program statewide by July 1986, the need for a more coordinated approach to service and assessment became evident. Struggles among the three primary service agencies at the county level mirrored those at the state level. There remained a great deal of suspicion that the Office on Aging and its local agencies were trying to consolidate all services to the aging under their jurisdiction. The original director of the State Office on Aging had publicly called for such consolidation on more than one occasion. The state's Department of Human Resources argued that all case management should be done in its local Departments of Social Services. At the same time within the DHMH there was a strong push for "Medicaiding" any program that could be modified to be eligible for federal matching funds. In addition, foreshadowing trends in the early 1990s, there were efforts in some counties to funnel public funds to allow private social services agencies to conduct evaluations and provide services. Baltimore City had a long tradition of referring clients to privately run social services agencies linked with various religious groups, for example. This combination of motives led to a series of committees and competing reports, eventually culminating in the creation of the STEPS preadmission screening process.

❖ STATEWIDE EVALUATION AND PLANNING SERVICES

In developing its preadmission screening process, Maryland built on the experience of CPP, GES, and Gateway II, as well as on other states' knowledge. By 1986, 27 other states had successfully implemented preadmission screening programs to divert admissions and reduce nursing home days. A committee of representatives from the state Health, Human Resources, and Aging agencies, supplemented by experienced local workers, met during 1985 and 1986 to design the system. Options papers were prepared by interested state-level entities.

According to the committee's options paper, the objectives being sought were the following:

1. Reduce inappropriate nursing facility use—nursing home beds had doubled in less than a decade and nursing facility care was more than 60% Medicaid-reimbursed.

2. Prepare for an expected statewide onslaught of older citizens given a predicted 200,000 increase in elderly population in 15 years.

3. Target evaluations to those most at risk of long-term institutionalization in order to use evaluation funds in the most cost-beneficial manner.

4. Tie improved availability of evaluations and care planning to increased community services at the local level.

5. Enable Medicaid to pay for evaluations and care planning using a uniform reporting tool statewide that would provide statewide information on functional disability levels and unmet need for community services—the data gathered would be used for program planning and analysis.

6. Encourage local agency coordination to avoid duplication of effort. Specifically, share intake information on new clients so that individuals would not have to be screened repeatedly to obtain each needed service.

7. Use existing agencies wherever possible—avoid creating new ones.

8. Maintain sufficient monitoring at the state level to ensure high quality evaluations and care planning delivered in a cost-efficient manner.

9. Maximize federal reimbursement for evaluations. (Alt, 1985)

Trying to meet all of these objectives, the committee finally developed the following eligibility and reporting criteria for the STEPS process. In order for the local assessment team's work to be reimbursed by Medicaid, the client had to meet medical and financial eligibility standards:

1. Medical eligibility: Medically, STEPS clients were to be adults who were either applying for nursing facility admission or who were found by the GES worker to be sufficiently frail that the utilization control agent also known as the Professional Review Organization (PRO) would likely find them medically eligible if they applied for certification.

2. Financial eligibility: Clients had to be either currently Medicaid-eligible or with a sufficiently low income that they would spend down to Medicaid eligibility within six months in a nursing facility (this was ascertained by client report, not by the Medical Assistance financial eligibility review process in the local Department of Social Services).

What the committee produced was a multipart carbonized form, crafted from assessment forms previously used at the local-level agencies and from national-level preadmission screening recommendations. Local agencies were free to add their additional pages to the form, to capture information that they felt was needed. The one-page summary sheet was submitted to the state Medicaid office for reimbursement and coding for planning use and was also intended to be shared among the local agencies for coordination purposes, as well as to decrease client time spent with repetitive intake procedures.

On the summary sheet were the following items:

1. Provider identification (which county's GES completed the evaluation).

2. Client identification: Name, address, referral source, referral reason, location during evaluation, date of birth, sex, race, marital status, permanent living arrangement, date admitted to nursing facility (if living in one), health insurance coverage, and primary source of health care.

3. Program information: Dates of referral, preliminary evaluation, and multidisciplinary assessment; evaluating agency; whether the client was hospitalized; and whether this was a reassessment.

4. Multidisciplinary assessment information: Has the client been officially PRO-certified for nursing home level of care and, if so, date of certification? Does the client meet medical eligibility requirements for STEPS evaluation? Is the client currently a Medicaid patient? If so, list Medicaid number. If not, is client STEPS financially eligible?

5.   Summary information: Total score on Activities of Daily Living (ADL disability rating); separate scores on dependence in Eating, Transferring, Dressing, Bathing, Toileting (these were the scores found in previous literature to be most indicative of long-term nursing facility use); Primary medical conditions present (up to three); Mental orientation.

6.   Recommendations: Up to six items in a plan of care; STEPS Case Management.

Maryland's state legislature during the 1986 session passed House Bill 522, creating the new STEPS program. STEPS evaluations began in October 1986, and permanent regulations governing the process went into effect on January 1, 1987. The numbers of individuals assessed under the program climbed steadily from 4,027 in fiscal year 1987 (July 1986 to June 1987) to 11,439 in fiscal year 1997.

❖   IMPLEMENTING THE STEPS PROCESS

In the beginning of the STEPS process, there was reluctance among some local county health department staffers over the course of an evaluation to inquire about clients' financial status in more detail than before. Previously, asking whether a client had a Medicaid number and what it was did not seem any more unusual than asking if they had any other form of insurance. Now, however, asking about a person's income and assets to determine his or her potential to "spend down" to Medicaid if in a nursing home felt much more intrusive. Staff was uncomfortable having to do it and had to be convinced of its importance to enable the local county health department to receive reimbursement from Medicaid for their work.

The planning committee had originally intended that the summary form be submitted for every GES client in order to gauge "unmet need" even though evaluations done on patients without medical or financial STEPS eligibility would not be reimbursable by Medicaid. GES staff had been used to operating on grant funding and not concerning themselves with reimbursement issues. Within a short time, GES staff stopped submitting STEPS forms to the state on clients whose evaluations were not likely to be eligible for reimbursement.

Meanwhile, another new task was added to the evaluation teams' workload with the federal requirement that states create systems for preadmission screening of mental patients seeking nursing facility care. It came into effect with the passage of the federal Omnibus Budget Reconciliation Act (OBRA) of 1987. After more state Health Department committee work, it was determined that the STEPS process could incorporate the new program as of 1989.

❖ ADDING PREADMISSION
SCREENING AND RESIDENT REVIEW

OBRA mandated that by January 1989 states implement PASRR. The act required that a nursing home certified for Medicare or Medicaid may not admit a patient who requires active treatment for mental illness or developmental disability. AERS/GES incorporated into its process Medicare/Medicaid-funded preadmission evaluations of any adult seeking nursing facility placement who was suspected of, or had a diagnosis of mental illness, developmental disability, or both. In addition to the existing STEPS evaluation for such patients, an in-depth psychiatric or psychological evaluation was conducted. AERS/GES also began conducting annual resident reviews of nursing facility residents with mental illness, developmental disability, or both. As appropriate, a psychiatrist or psychologist participated in these reviews. Because of the additional screening, these reviews were both more costly and less common than STEPS evaluations. However, these reviews built on GES's original expertise in psychiatric evaluations. In fiscal year 1997, there were 2,409 PASRR reviews done, at a total cost of

$1,006,605 (approximately $418 each), compared with 11,439 STEPS evaluations, at a total cost of $3,145,725 (approximately $275 each) (Maryland Department of Health and Mental Hygiene, 1999b).

❖ LEGAL AND TRAINING CONCERNS SHAPE STEPS

The Multi-Disciplinary Assessment section of the STEPS form contained six questions (Items 26 through 31) that were central to an evaluation's being reimbursable by Medicaid (see Appendix 5.2). These included two items (Items 26 and 27) inquiring about the client's status with the department's utilization review agent, the Delmarva Foundation (technically known as the PRO). Delmarva staff did a medical chart review of all nursing home admissions to determine if they qualified for Medicaid-funded care. The evaluator only had to copy this information from the patient's chart. There were also two items (Items 29 and 30) inquiring about whether a client was already a Medicaid recipient. If so, the evaluator could copy the Medicaid number from the person's card. Two other items (Items 28 and 31) turned out to be more difficult to interpret.

For the first eight years of assessments (1987 through 1994), close to 100% of the STEPS clients were rated as "yes" on Item 28, indicating that they either were already certified as needing nursing facility level of care or would need it if community-based long-term care were not available. However, when the form was changed in 1995 to include a third choice, "potentially eligible," there was an immediate drop in those ranked "yes." In 1995, the "yes" and "potential" answers were about evenly split at around 49% each. In 1996 and 1997, the "potential" category soared, while the "yes" answers dropped to 22% in 1997. "No" never received more than 1 to 2% of the answers.

Another way of examining these data is to look at the relationship between actual PRO certification and what the STEPS evaluation indicated. Overall during the 1988 to 1997 period, less than 3% of those already having been PRO-certified were given "potential" or "no" ratings by the STEPS evaluators. On the other hand, 24% of those not recorded as having been PRO-certified were given a "potentially eligible rating," and 75% were given a "yes" (definitely eligible) rating. Assuming that most of the "no" answers on the question about PRO certification meant that the clients had not been evaluated yet, rather than that they had been found ineligible, these results indicated that the STEPS workers were extremely confident that the clients being evaluated were at a level of frailty indicating a possible need for nursing home level of care.

Why would a "potential" category be needed? A lot depended on what the clients believed a STEPS evaluation proved. As the data above showed, there were a significant number of clients who had not been evaluated by Delmarva yet and a tiny number who had been turned down. The DHMH staff and nursing home administrators were concerned that people's hopes would be raised by the STEPS provider's indication of certifiability, then shattered by a Delmarva denial, potentially leading to lawsuits. Logically enough, after changing the form, the local workers were carefully trained to reconsider their choices and be sure to use "potential" if they were not positive about the client's status.

But what if the assessments *had* changed over time toward recommending less institutional plans of care for clients with levels of dependency and medical diagnoses that would previously have received recommendations for nursing home level of care? Was this a result of better availability of community services, of reduced citizen demand for nursing homes, or of more appropriate evaluations by STEPS providers, perhaps linked with better understanding of the Delmarva certification process and requirements?

❖   REPOSITIONING GES TO BECOME AERS

In 1999, the official name of the local Health Department evaluation services became Adult Evaluation and Review Services (AERS), replacing GES. GES remained as a central part of the service package, but the name change emphasized the organization's focus on a wide range of adults, including those in particular categories such as STEPS and PASRR clients. In their 30-year existence as GES and AERS, these evaluation units had moved full circle from being focused primarily on older persons seeking admission to a state mental facility, through adding evaluations for those seeking nursing home or community-based care including Adult Day Care and Adult Protective Services, to defining themselves in the 1999 brochure as follows. "AERS provides assistance to aged and functionally disabled adults who are at risk of institutionalization. AERS staff conducts a comprehensive evaluation to identify services available to help the individual to remain in the community, or in the least restrictive environment, while functioning at the highest possible level of independence and personal well-being" (Maryland Department of Health and Mental Hygiene, 1999a).

The services available by 1999 included GES services for those over 65 seeking admission to a state mental facility; STEPS for any adult at risk of nursing home placement; PASRR for those seeking nursing facility placement and suspected of, or with a diagnosis of, mental illness, developmental disability, or both. It also offered evaluations for other adults with functional difficulties seeking help to identify home- and community-based services, along with some limited case management services. All services were free except case management, which was covered for Medicaid recipients for a limited time. Others using AERS case management were charged on a sliding fee scale according to their ability to pay.

❖   GROWING INTEREST IN STEPS
    PROCESS FOR NEW PROGRAMS

As the availability of Medicaid waiver programs grew, along with an interest in Medicaid managed care, DHMH began reconsidering its programs. In 1994, it helped create and began contracting with the Center for Health Program Development and Management at the University of Maryland, Baltimore County. The center developed the federal applications for Medicaid waivers for Maryland's "HealthChoice" (managed care) and Children's Health Insurance Programs and was involved in the development of numerous other applications for waivered services programs. In the process of exploring the development of an integrated acute and long-term care "Social Health Maintenance Organization" program for older adults, the center examined the STEPS data in comparison with dually eligible citizens' Medicare information in order to decide whether to use the STEPS process for eligibility determination. Another academic group at the medical campus of the University of Maryland, Baltimore, explored the usefulness of the STEPS process in evaluating the medication management needs of individuals living in senior apartments in Baltimore City. In both cases, STEPS was found to be a promising source of information worth retaining rather than developing new screening tools.

❖ QUESTIONS REMAINING

Despite more than a decade of use as an evaluation and data collection tool, and as a path for reimbursement by Medicaid for local health departments, questions remained about STEPS. The results of the evaluations had shifted over time, while the expertise and commitment of the evaluation staffs at the local health departments had remained essentially the same. What should be the next steps in understanding the meaning and value of STEPS? Could the data be valuable for policy decisions in Maryland? Could it be extrapolated to other states? What other information should be gathered to put it in a more useful context? The students formed into small groups again to consider these questions.

APPENDIX 5.1

Chart 1   STEPS Assessment of Eligibility for Nursing Home Care, 1988–1997

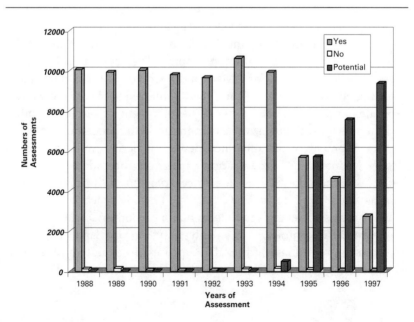

Chart 2   Most Common Recommendations in STEPS Plans of Care,
1988–1997

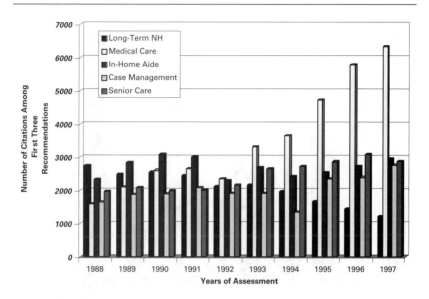

Chart 3   Primary Reasons for Referral for STEPS Assessment,
1988–1997

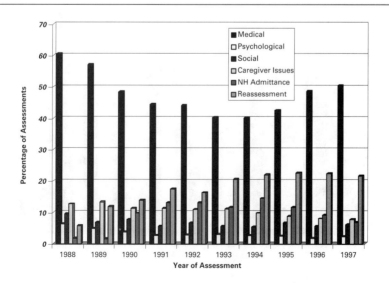

Chart 4   Reasons for Referral in Selected Maryland Counties,
1988–1997

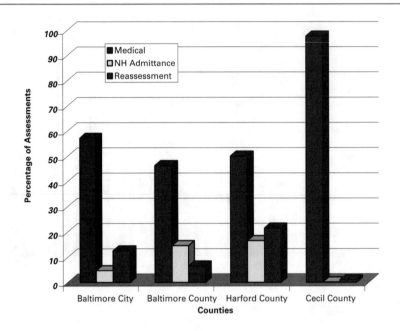

Chart 5   First Recommendation in STEPS Plans of Care in Selected
Maryland Counties, 1988–1997

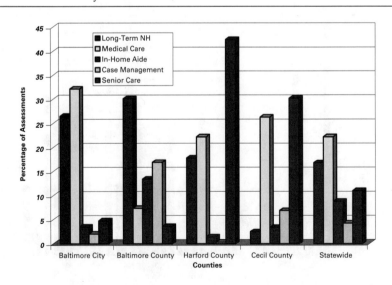

Chart 6   Levels of Reported Disability in Selected Maryland Counties, 1988–1997

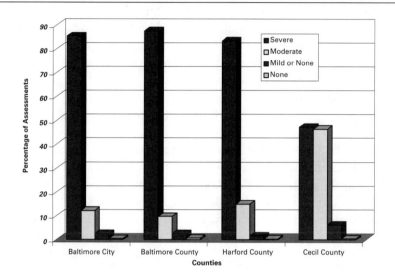

APPENDIX 5.2

Eligibility Questions on STEPS Summary Form

Item 26: "PRO certified for nursing facility care?" (Answered yes or no, indicated that the client had already been reviewed by the Delmarva Foundation for Medical Care, and found medically eligible.)

Item 27: "If yes, date." (Answered with the date the Delmarva certification took effect.) These posed little problem, as the GES worker could simply copy the information from the patient's chart.

Item 28: Client meets COMAR 10.09.30.01B(09) requirements? (Answered originally yes or no, later a "potential" category was added.) The form included the following paragraph on the coding sheet to assist the workers in answering it.

"A STEPS Medically Eligible client is (a) person: 'Who is certified by the Department or its designee as requiring nursing home care under the Program (Medicaid) pursuant to COMAR 10.09.10 Skilled Nursing Facility Services or 10.09.11 Intermediate Care Facility Services, or who, as determined by the STEPS provider based on the data collected in the comprehensive evaluation requires services consistent with the Program's (Medicaid's) description of the level of care and type of services rendered in the comprehensive care facilities reim-bursed under the Program, including participants who would require inpatient care if community based long term care services were not available; and (b) Whose disabilities and needs cannot be adequately met in an episodic ambulatory care setting but who requires continu-ing institutional or community based long term care services."

Item 29: "Is client currently active Medicaid?" (Answered yes or no, indicating current enrollment in the program.)

Item 30: "If yes, MA #." (Spaces left for the official Medicaid number.)

Item 31: "If no, is client STEPS financially eligible?" (Answered yes, no, or not applicable.) GES workers were given a regularly updated sheet indicating the upper limit on income and assets the client would need in order to qualify for Medicaid either immediately or within six months in a nursing facility. As this was self-reported, it caused little problem, other than worker reluctance to embarrass clients by asking it.

❖   REFERENCES

Alt, P. M. (1985). *Options paper on implementing pre-admission screening.* Unpublished report for the Maryland Interagency Committee on Aging Services.

Alt, P. M. (1998). Future directions for public senior services: Meeting diverg-ing needs. *Generations, 22,* 29–33.

Justice, D. (1988). *State long-term care reform: Development of community care sys-tems in six states.* Washington, DC: Center for Policy Research, National Governors' Association.

Maryland Department of Budget and Fiscal Planning. (1984). *Review and comparison of four in-home service programs.* Unpublished report to the Maryland General Assembly.

Maryland Department of Health and Mental Hygiene, Geriatric Evaluation Services Program. (1985). *Pre-admission screening proposal.* Unpublished report for the Maryland Interagency Committee on Aging Services.

Maryland Department of Health and Mental Hygiene, Medical Care Programs. (1985). *STEPS: Statewide Evaluation and Planning Services.* Unpublished report for the Maryland Interagency Committee on Aging Services.

Maryland Department of Health and Mental Hygiene, Medical Care Programs. (1999a). *Adult evaluation and review services.* Brochure.

Maryland Department of Health and Mental Hygiene, Medical Care Programs. (1999b). *Maryland medical assistance program: The year in review, fiscal year 1997*. Baltimore: Maryland Department of Health and Mental Hygiene.

Simpson, D. F. (1986). *Gateway II and long term care in Maryland*. Unpublished report for the Maryland Interagency Committee on Aging Services.

6

Teaching What They Practice

Carole L. Jurkiewicz

"We've hired an office manager to deal with those types of problems. They're not my responsibility. If you have a dental or student question, feel free to come to me. If not, go see Deidre." This was the oft-stated position of Dr. Corbett, clinical supervisor.

Renee, a faculty member, frustrated by what she perceived were legal, ethical, and moral violations in this dental clinic of a large technical college, had gone to see Deidre on many occasions. No matter what the violation or seriousness of the infraction, Deidre stated that she was simply too busy with her regular duties as office manager to concern herself with the practice of medicine. "Go see Dr. Corbett; he's the clinical supervisor. It's his problem, not mine. Maybe if he hired an assistant for me I would have the time to help you out. You can tell him I said that too."

Deidre had worked her way up from receptionist to office manager over the seventeen years she had worked for Dr. Corbett and had seen many assistant professors like Renee come and go. "They think they're going to change the world but it isn't going to start here. I've been here long before they came and will be here long after they're gone." Deidre's style of communication, perceived by others as blunt and many times insubordinate, had never been directly addressed by Dr. Corbett, who commented he was concerned about a lawsuit because she was the only minority in the department. Deidre had, on many occasions, drawn attention to the fact that there were no African American professors hired into the department, and Dr. Corbett viewed these comments as a form of ethnic activism which, he claimed, he wanted to avoid. At sixty-three, Dr. Corbett was reaching the end of his career and had been reducing both the number of hours worked and the amount of work done while in his office. He was frequently away on travel with his wife and left the running of the clinic to whoever wanted to take charge. The perception of others in the office was that he was already effectively retired but was holding on to his position for the financial benefits it bestowed upon him.

❖   LACK OF LEADERSHIP

In her role as chair of the Ethics Committee, Renee was responsible for gathering information on the anonymous complaints received, and presenting it to either the clinical supervisor or the office manager for resolution. Her committee of five (herself, two students, the human resource manager, and an associate professor of radiology) met only when a complaint was received in the box outside Renee's office. Since becoming chair of the committee, Renee had investigated the nine complaints she had received by following the protocol established years ago: convene the committee appointed by the clinical supervisor, solicit their help in collecting the information necessary to substantiate the complaint, and present the findings in a report.

There were no written guidelines for the committee, only the procedural list verbally given to Renee by the previous chair when she arrived. Members of the Ethics Committee received no compensation or credit for time spent in committee meetings or on committee work. Often, members of her committee did not attend the meetings, and the responsibility for collecting the data fell primarily on her alone. No action had been taken on any of her reports, nor on any of the reports compiled by the committee before her arrival. Her work on the committee was seen as tangential to her other duties, and she was not evaluated on her work as chair. The process and the committee were generally viewed as an unnecessary function that nonetheless lent credibility to the practice. On a few occasions, the Ethics Committee had been lauded in the media by the college president, using it as an example of the integrity of the institution.

Renee had tried nearly since her arrival two years ago to call attention to the serious problems she saw in the practice. As an untenured faculty member she did not feel she could pursue these problems as vigorously as she would like, for fear of endangering her career. "But I can't simply ignore them. We are putting patients in danger, we are in violation of OSHA[1] (Occupational Safety and Health Administration) rulings, we are in violation of the American Dental Association[2] guidelines, and we are frankly operating in an unethical manner. No one seems to be concerned but me. If I seek formal resolution to these problems I will almost certainly be refused tenure and could lose my job and career. If nothing is done and the violations are discovered, we will likely be sued and as an untenured faculty member and chair of the Ethics Committee, the finger will certainly point to me. I could lose my job either way. If only I could find out a way to make them listen."

❖ VIOLATIONS AT THE CLINIC

Renee's frustration with this role had increased over time. Some of the violations, in her opinion, "are not all that serious and if nothing is done about them I don't think any harm will result. Grade inflation, not respecting patient confidentiality, and theft of supplies like toothbrushes, floss, fluoride rinse, and bleaching gel are not to be condoned but are not matters of life and death. Others are putting us in violation of laws that could result in fines, imprisonment, and the closing of our facility. The worst case is the latest one. We are actually killing our patients and no one will do anything about it! I've decided to put my biggest concerns in writing to protect myself if word of this situation leaks out. If the person who reported it to me goes public, I'm going to be ready with the documentation to protect myself and my job. If my career or tenure is threatened, I have no other choice."

Renee made duplicate copies of every complaint and investigative report since her arrival at the college and kept them at her home. She also made copies of the complaints filed before she arrived to the extent she could locate them. After consulting with an attorney friend, she compiled detailed records of her meetings with the clinical supervisor and office manager stating the day, time, location of the meeting, topic of conversation, and outcome of the meeting. When possible, she followed the meeting with a memo to both outlining the content and result of the meeting and kept a copy for her records.

"I noticed in reviewing these complaints that there is something more important at stake than the individual violation. There is a pattern of legal and ethical misconduct that is not only an accepted part of our practice, but is the example we are teaching our students on how their practices should be run. When we do wrong, it is multiplied hundreds if not thousands of times by the consequences to our students as well as our patients. This is not a place where I want to work any longer. I've decided to see what opportunities are on the job market and hope to be gone within a year or two. I'm wondering if I should just take this evidence to the media now, in order to protect our patients, rather than waiting for someone else to blow the whistle. I don't know if I can just keep quiet and let this go on." Of the reports Renee compiled, five instances stood out as being the most potentially damaging, the last of which gave her the greatest cause for concern. She reread these complaints, printed below (with edits only for grammar and to protect confidentiality), thinking what her next steps should be.

Complaint 1: Inadequate Supervision of Student Practitioners

"The dentist we employ part-time as a supervising dentist has his own practice separate from our college. He is frequently arriving late to work at our clinic because of his practice and generally leaves our facility before the last patient has been released. As you know, we are required by the State Board of Dentistry to run the clinic under direct supervision. This means a licensed dentist must be physically present in the clinic while the hygienist, whether a student or a licensed professional, is working on a client. When I refuse to allow them to do anything other than take vital signs or provide oral hygiene instruction until this dentist arrives, he becomes angry, yells at me in front of the students and the clients, and says they can start without him as his employees do it all the time. He then apologizes to the student practitioners saying he is sorry I made them wait and that they will now not have enough time to complete their daily assignments because of me. The students then get angry at me and usually rush their patients through without adequate care so they can get their grade for the day."

Complaint 2: Impaired Dentists Reporting for Work

"It is sometimes necessary to schedule makeup clinics in the evenings because of equipment failure or professional cancellations. The supervising dentist for these evening sessions frequently schedules a round of golf before his evening shift at our clinic and arrives with a strong smell of alcohol on his breath, glassy eyes, slurred speech, and an inability to walk normally. The American Dental Association has published strict guidelines on the obligation professionals have to report impaired colleagues and to ensure that the patients are protected. When I refuse to let this supervising dentist see patients in his condition, he becomes angry at me and begins threatening me. I have secluded him in the radiology viewing area in these circumstances where he usually sleeps until the shift is over. I cannot let him leave as we must have a licensed dentist on the premises, even if he is impaired, in order for the clinic to be able to offer services."

Complaint 3: Broken Instrument Pieces Left in Patient's Mouth

"A second-year dental hygiene student under the supervision of Dr. Wright was working on a rather difficult patient when her instrument tip fractured off under the tissue near tooth number three. She could not see it and her exploration for the broken tip only aggravated the patient further. The student became visibly distraught and asked if she could speak to Dr. Wright away from the patient. When she told him what happened, he informed her to leave it there. He said the radiograph necessary to locate the instrument piece, and the surgery to remove it, would be too expensive and they could not charge it to the patient without explaining what happened. Also, this patient was a difficult one and would likely sue the clinic for malpractice. He said it was unlikely to cause the patient significant harm and that if there was trouble, the patient would not be able to say when the problem occurred. The patient left the office with a broken instrument tip embedded in his tissue."

Complaint 4: Intentional Overexposure of Client to X Rays

"Students are overexposing their patients to radiation in order to improve their grades in radiology. Policies in place to protect the patient state that only three X ray retakes are allowed for a series of eighteen films, and one retake for a series of four films. This is the maximum allowable amount of exposure to radiation for an individual without causing damage.[3] There is little or no supervision of students in the radiology area as instructors are usually in the clinical area with patients. Students have access to virtually unlimited stores of X ray film. In violation of the allowable number of exposures, students are doing eight to ten retakes on a series of eighteen films and two to three on a series of four films. They submit the best X rays for grading and discard the rest, thereby increasing their grade but threatening the life of the patient in the process. Patients are generally unaware of the dangers involved in exposure to radiation through dental X rays and the subsequent potential for serious damage to the brain and soft tissue of the head and neck. When patients ask about the number of X rays being taken they are told the equipment is malfunctioning. Students say taking multiple X rays is a common practice and one encouraged by their professors."

Complaint 5: Improper Sterilization and Patient Infection

"The Sterilization Center of our clinic, although aesthetically designed, is not in compliance with OSHA rulings and violates the mandatory Infection Control Program. As a result of our physical layout (see Figure 6.1), unsterilized instruments are being used on patients resulting in high rates of HIV, hepatitis, and viral infections amongst our clients. Activities to be performed in the Sterilization Center include recirculating of contaminated instruments through cleaning, drying, wrapping, sterilizing, labeling, and storing of instruments. OSHA requirements state that each Sterilization Center have a clearly designated "clean" and "dirty" area to eliminate cross-contamination.

"The design of our Sterilization Center has two key flaws: (a) lack of counter space places the "clean" and "dirty" instruments in close proximity; (b) the area is not secured and is used as a pass-through area for faculty, students, and sometimes patients. Given that we have a busy practice by any measure, and that the faculty and students practicing in our clinic are here for only short periods of time and are not well-acquainted with the layout, we have documented that in nearly one-half of the cases "dirty" instruments are being used on patients. This has resulted in substantiated cases of certain strains of HIV, hepatitis, and viral infections spread to patients in our clinic. In addition,

Figure 6.1   Diagram of the Dental Office

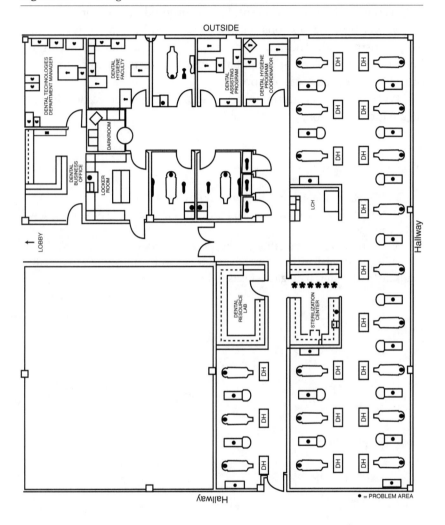

people passing through that area are unintentionally dirtying those instruments that are sterile through inadvertent touch or coughing, and on occasion have cut themselves on contaminated instruments when bumping into the countertop.

"The office manager has refused to reorganize the Sterilization Center to prevent this from occurring and, instead, has taken to wearing protective gloves even in her office. The clinical supervisor says it is the office manager's responsibility, that he has trust in her judgment, and that to change anything now would be an admission of our guilt in infecting patients to this point. He has ordered me to keep quiet and to conduct training sessions on OSHA universal precautions and disease transmission. The infection rates of our patients are becoming known amongst some area dentists who have refused to continue in our employ for fear of infection."

With the reports sitting on her desk, Renee needed to decide now on a course of action.

❖ NOTES

1.   OSHA guidelines can be found at www.osha.gov/

2.   ADA Code of Ethics can be found at www.ada.org/prof/prac/law/code/code.pdf

3. Information on radiation exposure and dental X rays can be found at www.physics.isu.edu/radinf/dental.htm and http://www.uvm.edu/~radsafe/newsletter/biological.effects.50.html

7

The Edifice Complex

A New Coliseum for Charlotte?

Terrel L. Rhodes and Linda E. Swayne

Charlotte's City Council met weekly on Monday nights, but this was a special meeting with only one item on the agenda: the new arena proposal. Was Charlotte going to invest millions of dollars in a new arena? It was getting late. Most of the evening had been devoted to citizens who stated their views for or against a new arena. Although every councilmember listened to the expressed views, ultimately the decision was the council's responsibility. The council had several options: They could vote to build a new arena with public funds; they could partner with the Charlotte Hornets of the National Basketball Association (NBA) and share the costs of a new arena; they could place a referendum on the ballot so the citizens could vote directly on the issue; or they could do nothing and most likely lose the Hornets to another city. None of the options was without risks. A referendum was one option perceived by the councilmembers as a possible way for them to avoid having to take a direct stand on the new arena and thus be able to escape the political backlash from those who were dissatisfied with the outcome of the referendum. However, a referendum would delay construction for another year and the Hornets might decide to leave Charlotte. It was time for the councilmembers to speak.

"Spending $200 million of taxpayer dollars for a new arena is a waste. Spending $30,000 to educate the people of this city about the arena is ludicrous. I would like to see the $30,000 going to drug education. We should spend $30,000 to sort of soften up the citizens of this city so this city can spend $200 million for one industry that was out of business half of the year [referring to the NBA strike that caused one-half of the 1998–1999 season to be cancelled] and the city got no rent whatsoever?" said Al Rousso, a city council-member elected at-large.

"It stretches beyond any normal definition of a public service," agreed Mike Jackson, the representative of District 7.

"I am astonished at the arena backers' insistence on thwarting the will of the people," said Don Reid, another at-large councilmember. Reid was referring to the November 1997 *Charlotte Observer*/ WCNC-TV poll that found 64% of the area residents polled (and 56% who said they were Hornets' followers) said they would not support spending public money to help build an arena. The news-paper/TV research group polled 404 people aged 18 and over between November 20 and 22, 1997. The maximum sampling error was ± 4.9 percentage points. For a subset of 233 who identified themselves as following the Hornets, the sampling error was ± 6.4 percentage points.

"The data around the country in terms of public support for sports facilities is not only strongly favorable, but unanimously favor-able," pointed out Del Borgsdorf, deputy city manager. "The Hornets have added substantially to the Authority's revenues and the fans have come to Charlotte for games and spent their hard-earned dollars." The Auditorium-Coliseum-Convention Center Authority (the Authority) was charged with overseeing the public venues owned by the City of Charlotte: Ovens Auditorium, Independence Arena (the old coliseum now used for the Charlotte Checkers East Coast Hockey League team), the Charlotte

Coliseum (nicknamed the "Hive" for the Hornets), the old convention center (vacant since 1998), and the new convention center. The Authority had responsibility for the management and operation of the five properties, making reasonable rules and regulations, and establishing and collecting rents and fees for their use.

"George Shinn [Hornets owner] needs to put more on the table. Right now, the deal presented is not the best one for the taxpayer," commented Lynn Wheeler, mayor pro tem. She continued, "I realize the Hornets have done a lot for this city, but if we build a new arena in the uptown area, what will we do with the Hive and Independence Arena?"

"And, how are we going to pay for it?" asked Don Reid. "I am totally opposed to raising taxes and the poll shows that most citizens don't want any public funding."

There had been many meetings, extensive discussion, and a number of public forums to listen to citizen input—both for and against a new arena. The city council had appointed a citizen committee to advise them on this hotly debated topic. The committee was ready to make its final report to the council. Each councilmember knew it was an important political decision if they wanted to be reelected. Should they vote for or against public involvement in a new arena for Charlotte? If they voted "for," what should that public involvement include?

❖ CHARLOTTE—THE CITY

Charlotte was the largest city in both Carolinas and in 1999 had a population of 512,628; the Charlotte metropolitan statistical area contained 1.4 million people and more than 6.0 million people lived within a 100-mile radius of the city.

Economic Boom

Centrally located in the state of North Carolina at the South Carolina border, the city was a major financial center. The corporate headquarters of Bank of America, First Union, and Wachovia attracted other financial services including accounting firms, insurance companies, and law practices. Charlotte was a passenger hub for USAirways. Other major companies with significant presence included IBM, AT&T, DuPont, Coca Cola Bottling, Royal and SunAlliance Insurance, TransAmerica Reinsurance, TIAA-CREF, and Duke Energy.

Charlotte's population grew 19.6% between 1980 and 1990 and grew another 16.2% between 1990 and 1997. Its growth was fueled by the influx of both companies and people to the Sunbelt. The unemployment rate in 1999 hovered around 3%. The per capita income was $25,446 (1996 data, latest available).

In 1999, in addition to the Hornets, Charlotte was the home of NASCAR, World Wrestling Federation, the Carolina Panthers (NFL), the Knights (AAA baseball), and the Checkers (minor league hockey). The professional sports entrée, however, had been through the NBA and the Hornets.

Financial Condition

The city received the Certificate of Achievement for Excellence in Financial Reporting in 1996 for the clarity and completeness of its presentation of budget information (see Exhibit 7.1 for the city's financial policies). Charlotte's General Obligation bonds were rated Aaa (since 1973) by Moody's Investor Service and AAA (since 1976) by Standard & Poor's (see Exhibits 7.2 and 7.3 for a summary of the city's debt). Charlotte was one of 25 cities that had Aaa/AAA ratings by both agencies. The ratings were based on the strength of the local economy, the diversity of that economy, and the financial management of the city over time.

Exhibit 7.1   City of Charlotte Financial Policies, Fiscal Year 1999

City Council's Capital Investment Plan financial policies are as follows:

1. General government debt policies:

   - Diversify revenue sources dedicated to capital formation and debt service.

- Maintain a balanced mix of financing strategies for funding capital projects without an excessive reliance on any one source. Examples of financing strategies include pay-as-you-go, grants, and debt.

- Provide for issuance of additional debt at reasonable time intervals without increasing taxes, and timed in such a way as to avoid erratic impacts on tax rate changes.

- Maintain the highest credit rating by scheduling and issuing debt that sustains reasonable ratios (e.g., percent of outstanding debt to assessed value).

2. The dedication of specific revenues to the capital plan will be maintained in the Municipal Debt Service Fund. In fiscal year 1999, the specific revenues dedicated to the Municipal Debt Service Fund include the following:

- 6.7 cents of the property tax rate;

- A portion of the city's proceeds from the occupancy tax;

- Investment (interest) income;

- 0.5 cent sales tax; and

- Other/miscellaneous revenues including a portion of the intangibles tax, ABC profits, beer and wine license revenues, and a contribution from Mecklenburg county for its share of debt cost for the Charlotte-Mecklenburg Government Center.

3. Municipal Debt Service Fund Balance will be maintained at an adequate level to cover debt costs. The ratio of debt service fund balance to actual debt service costs will approximate 50%.

4. Pay-As-You-Go Tax Fund will be used in conjunction with long-term debt financing to finance capital projects.

5. Asset sales will be dedicated to the Capital Investment Plan. The retirement of any outstanding debt on sold assets will be the first priority of sales proceeds.

6. Enterprise Fund's capital plans will be established on a self-sustaining basis (water and sewer and airport).

(Continued)

Exhibit 7.1 Continued

- Water and sewer and airport capital projects are financed from revenues generated from user fees and charges.

- The water/sewer rate study assumes maintenance of debt service coverage as required in Revenue bond financing documents.

- Storm water is scheduled to become a self-sustaining Enterprise Fund in FY2001, at which time it will rely solely on storm water fees and charges.

The City of Charlotte's Pay-As-You-Go and Capital Policy

Each year, during the budget process, the city council dedicates 2.25 cents of the property tax rate for "pay-as-you-go" capital projects. The fund provides cash for relatively small capital projects. The fund along with the current contributions from the General Fund and proceeds from property sales maintains the financial policy of diversified revenue sources for the Capital Investment Plan.

Five-year totals from these revenues are as follows:

- $49 million from property tax;

- $17 million from general fund surplus;

- $1.2 million from property sales;

- $7.9 million from revenues; and

- $3.0 million from private contributions.

Source: City of Charlotte documents.

Exhibit 7.2   City of Charlotte General Obligation Debt, December 31, 1998

General Obligation Debt

General Government	$350,688,000
Water	245,648,000
Sewer	316,734,000
Airport	22,075,000
Total	$935,145,000

Authorized and Unissued General Obligation Bonds

Water/Sewer	$37,000,000
Street/Sidewalk	144,675,000
Neighborhood Improvement	12,000,000
Environmental Remediation	17,680,000
Total	$211,355,000

Summary of Annual Debt Service

	FY1999 Budget
General Government	$50,900,000
Water/Sewer	56,300,000
Aviation	26,100,000
Convention Center	13,000,000
Total	$146,300,000

Source: City of Charlotte documents.

Exhibit 7.3   City of Charlotte Non-General Obligation Debt, December 31, 1998

Funded by Specific Revenues

Airport Revenue Bonds	$166,650,000
Airport Special Facilities	86,612,000
Water/Sewer Revenue Bonds	60,185,000
Parking Deck Bonds	14,665,000
Subtotal	$328,112,000

Funded by General Revenue

Law Enforcement Facilities	20,845,000
Equipment Leases	19,365,000
Subtotal	40,210,000

Funded by Special Taxes

Convention Center	178,379,000
Total	$546,701,000

Source: City of Charlotte documents.

City Governance

The City of Charlotte was run by a council/manager form of government with a "weak" mayor and an eleven-member city council. In a council/manager form of government, the city council is elected and becomes the primary policy-making body. The council then hires a full-time professional manager to oversee operations of the city on a day-to-day basis. Charlotte was one of the first cities in North Carolina to have a professional city manager. The City of Charlotte was recognized by the International City Manager's Association as a well-administered city with a professional staff and culture for conducting the people's business. Charlotte had no major political scandals in its history until the 1999 conviction of the director of the board of elections for taking kickbacks on voting machine contracts.

A mayor is elected to represent the city at official functions, but the office has little formal authority although substantial ceremonial and public relations authority (see Exhibit 7.4 for information on each of the elected city officials, and Exhibit 7.5 for council district locations). The councilmembers were elected every two years in November. The mayor and four councilmembers were elected at-large by a city-wide vote. Seven councilmembers were elected from districts by voters who resided in the district.

Exhibit 7.4   Charlotte City Council

Mayor Patrick McCrory, a Republican, was elected to his first term as a member of the Charlotte City Council in 1989 and served as mayor pro tem from 1993–1995. He was elected mayor of Charlotte in November 1995 and was reelected in 1997 with 78% of the vote. During his second term, Mayor McCrory worked to increase resources to the criminal justice system, encouraged redevelopment in inner-city areas, and prepared for implementation of a 20-year Transit Plan for the Charlotte region. McCrory was considered to be a moderate Republican with a high level of energy and commitment to advancing the city both economically and socially as a place to live and to do business. Most local civic leaders and commentators believed McCrory would seek higher political office in the future. Mayor McCrory served as a part-time mayor and was employed by Duke Energy Corporation since

(*Text continues on page 115*)

1978 and was manager of business relations. Mayor McCrory graduated from Catawba College in 1978 with a bachelor's degree in political science/education.

Lynn Wheeler, a Republican, was mayor pro tem for the City of Charlotte. Wheeler was a councilmember elected at-large. She had served on the City Council of Charlotte for eight years—four years representing District 6 [see Exhibit 7.5 for map of district boundaries] and four years as an at-large representative. She was elected mayor pro tem in December 1997 by virtue of receiving the highest number of votes among the at-large candidates. Wheeler chaired the city council's Budget Committee and its Economic Development and Planning Committee and was a member of the Public Safety Committee. Before her first election in 1989, she served on the Charlotte-Mecklenburg Planning Commission for four years, as vice-chair of the commission and chair of the zoning committee. Wheeler was considered a moderate Republican committed to the economic development of the city. A homemaker, she had attended Hollins College.

Al Rousso, a Democrat, represented Charlotte City Council at-large. Rousso first was elected to the city council in 1985 and served for two terms before losing mayoral bids in 1989 and 1991. He was reelected to city council is 1995 and was serving his second consecutive term. Rousso chaired the Council-Manager Relations Committee, cochaired the Transportation Committee, and served on the City Council Budget Committee. Councilmember Rousso owned Brownlee Jewelers, Inc., for 54 years. He was considered a maverick councilmember who frequently championed the views of the "average" taxpayer in the community. Rousso was a graduate of Sidney Lanier High School in Montgomery, Alabama.

Don Reid, a Republican, represented Charlotte City Council at-large. He was first elected to office in 1991 and was serving his fourth consecutive term. Reid chaired the City Council Public Safety Committee, was vice-chair of the Restructuring Government Committee, and a member of the Council Budget Committee. Councilmember Reid owned Reid Associates, Inc., an advertising agency he founded in 1978. Reid was considered by himself and others to be a very conservative Republican.

(Continued)

Exhibit 7.4 Continued

He was a founding member of a grassroots community organization—Citizens for Effective Government—that consistently opposed government spending projects that might increase taxes or interfere with budget reductions. Reid was a graduate of Davidson College with a bachelor's degree in economics.

Rod Autrey, a Republican, represented Charlotte City Council at-large. He was serving his first term as a city councilmember. He was elected on a platform advocating an open and public review of the coliseum issue. He was a member of the Mecklenburg County Board of Commissioners for four terms and was its chair from 1990–1992. Autrey chaired the City Council City-Within-A-City Committee and was a member of the Budget and Transportation Committees. He was considered a moderate who tried to balance neighborhood interests with economic development in the city. Autrey was partner and client development director for Freeman White, Inc., a public accounting firm, and a graduate of the University of North Carolina—Chapel Hill.

Sara Spencer, a Democrat, represented Charlotte City Council District 1. She was first elected to public office in 1993 and was serving her third consecutive term. She was the cochair of the City Council Transportation Committee and served on the City-Within-A-City and Restructuring Government Committees. Spencer was an instructor in music at Central Piedmont Community College and performed locally. She was considered a liberal Democrat strongly linked with neighborhood activists. Councilmember Spencer received her bachelor's degree from Oberlin College and her master's degree from the Union Theological Seminary.

Malachi Greene, a Democrat, represented Charlotte City Council District 2. He was first elected to city council in 1995 and was serving his second consecutive term. He served on the City Council Economic Development-Planning, Council-Manager Relations, Transportation, and Restructuring Government Committees. Councilmember Greene served on the board and was chair of the Policy Committee of the National Black Caucus of Local Elected Officials. He was a moderate Democrat who generally supported economic development projects as long as they benefited, or at least did not adversely effect, the North Side areas he represented. Councilmember Greene was a real estate investor. He received his bachelor's degree from Livingstone College.

Patrick Cannon, a Democrat, represented Charlotte City Council District 3. He was elected to the Charlotte City Council in 1993 and was serving a third consecutive term. He was a member of the city council's Public Safety, City-Within-A-City, Budget, and Council-Manager Relations Committees. He was active in the National Black Caucus of Local Elected Officials. He generally supported neighborhood activists versus big banking interests, and paid particular attention to the impact of policy decisions on the West Side areas he represented. Councilmember Cannon was the owner and president of a parking design and management company, E-Z Parking. Cannon attended North Carolina A&T State University in Greensboro, NC, where he pursued a degree in communications and business management. He also attended the University of North Carolina at Chapel Hill.

Nasif Majeed, a Democrat, represented Charlotte City Council District 4. He was first elected to office in 1991 and was serving his fourth consecutive term. He was vice-chair of the City Council Economic Development-Planning Committee, vice-chair of the Public Safety Committee, and member of the Council-Manager Relations Committee. In addition to public service, Majeed was a past member of the Charlotte Housing Authority and the Charlotte-Mecklenburg Planning Commission. Majeed was a conservative Democrat who frequently supported economic development projects, especially if they benefited the minority residents in his district. He was a contract chaplain for the North Carolina Department of Corrections as well as president of Atlantic Distribution Company, a food distributorship. Majeed received his bachelor's and master's degrees from North Carolina A&T State University in Greensboro.

Tim Sellers, a Republican, represented Charlotte City Council District 5. He was first elected to office in 1995, and was serving his second consecutive term. He served on the city council's Economic Development-Planning, Council-Manager Relations, City-Within-A-City, and Public Safety Committees. He tended to

(Continued)

Exhibit 7.4 Continued

support economic development initiatives in the city but was very attentive to the impact of projects on taxes and the budget. Sellers was a partner with DeLaney and Sellers PA, Attorneys at Law, and was licensed in both North and South Carolina. Sellers received his undergraduate degree in economics from Davidson College in 1977 and received his juris doctorate with honors in 1980 from the University of North Carolina Law School in Chapel Hill.

Charles Baker, a Republican, represented Charlotte City Council District 6. First elected to office in 1993, Baker was serving his third consecutive term. Baker chaired the Restructuring Government Committee and served on the Economic Development-Planning Committee. He also represented the city with the Centralina Council of Governments. Baker was a past vice-chair of the Charlotte/Douglas International Airport Advisory Committee and past chair of the North Carolina Environmental Management Commission. He was generally skeptical about city spending beyond basic infrastructure and services. Councilmember Baker had been a senior consultant with HDR engineering since 1962. He held a bachelor's degree in civil engineering from The Citadel and a masters degree in environmental engineering from North Carolina State University.

Mike Jackson, a Republican, represented Charlotte City Council District 7. He was first elected to the Charlotte City Council in 1993. He was serving his third consecutive term. Jackson was the vice-chair of the City Council City-Within-A-City Committee and served on the Transportation and Restructuring Government Committees. He was the city's representative to the Arts and Science Council Board. He was stridently opposed to most economic development projects beyond basic roads, water, and sewer. Jackson was owner of Jackson's Java, Inc., and American Quest, Inc., home builders. Jackson was a graduate of the United States Military Academy, where he majored in engineering.

Exhibit 7.5   Charlotte City Council Districts, 1998

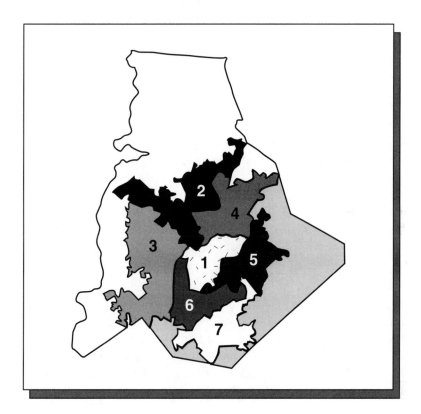

Although the at-large councilmembers were elected by all registered voters in the city and district representatives were elected only by registered voters within a specific district, all city council-members in practice tried to work together to provide policy decisions that benefited the community as a whole and provided quality service to all of Charlotte's districts. The councilmembers frequently met with the residents of the community by attending public functions and community meetings. Together, the mayor and the city councilmembers were responsible for establishing the general policies under which the city operated. These included

- appointing the city manager, city attorney, city clerk, and members of various boards and commissions;
- enacting ordinances, resolutions, and orders;
- reviewing the annual budget, setting tax rates, and approving the financing of all city operations; and
- authorizing contracts on behalf of the city.

The mayor presided at all of the city council meetings and officially represented the city at special ceremonies and events. Part of the mayor's duties included limited authority to appoint individuals to various boards and commissions and to be involved in national and international organizations that worked on issues important to Charlotte and the region. The mayor pro tem was elected by a vote of the city councilmembers. She or he assumed all duties, powers, and obligations of the Office of the Mayor in the mayor's absence, and would fill his term if for any reason the mayor could not continue in that role.

City Manager's Office. The city employed a full-time professional city manager as its key administrative officer to run the day-to-day operations of the city. Pamela A. Syfert, a long-time city employee and former budget director, was appointed city manager in September 1996 when Wendell White retired after a fifteen-year career as city manager (see Exhibit 7.6 for City of Charlotte organizational chart).

Volunteer Boards and Commissions. The City of Charlotte had 36 boards or commissions that were appointed by the city council from among self-nominations submitted to the city clerk's office. For example, the Airport Advisory Committee, the Civil Service Board, the Historic Landmarks Commission, the Planning Commission, and the Authority were appointed by the city council and reported to it.

The Authority. The Authority was deemed a "special district" as defined by North Carolina state statute. The seven-member governing board of the Authority was made up of two appointees by the mayor and five by the city council. The City of Charlotte paid the Authority's outstanding general obligation bonded debt, and any net

Exhibit 7.6   Charlotte City Government

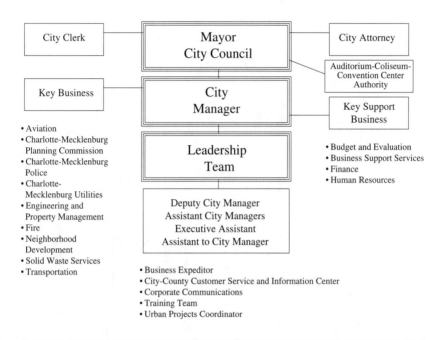

Source: City of Charlotte documents—budget report.

operating proceeds of the Authority were used to pay interest and principal on the bonded debt, or as otherwise directed by the city council. The city was financially accountable for an organization if it appointed a majority of the organization's governing body, if the city was able to impose its will on the organization, or if there was potential for the organization to provide specific financial benefits to, or impose specific financial burdens on, the city. Organizations for which the city was financially accountable were termed component units. As a component unit, the Authority was included in the city's financial statements as a discretely presented unit (see Exhibit 7.7 for Charlotte's Combined Balance Sheet, and Exhibit 7.8 for its Combined Statement of Revenues, Expenditures, and Changes in Fund Balances for 1998).

Exhibit 7.7 City of Charlotte, North Carolina, Combined Balance Sheet

Assets and Other Debits	General	Governmental Fund Types Special Revenue	Debt Service	Capital Projects	Totals (Memorandum Only) Primary Government	Auditorium-Coliseum-Convention Center Authority Component Unit
Current assets:						
Cash & cash equivalents/investments	$89,464	$41,120	$62,787	$68,074	$714,992	$11,766
Total current assets	114,820	49,316	65,910	73,211	799,727	13,865
Total restricted assets			16,288	7,068	110,708	
Total fixed assets, net					2,459,537	
Other debits:						
Amount available in Debt Service Fund					81,410	
Amount to be provided for retirement of general long-term debt					454,495	
Total assets and other debts	$115,317	$76,593	$82,198	$96,000	$3,954,828	$13,865
Liabilities, Equity and Other Credits						
Liabilities:						
Total current liabilities	13,746	5,138	42	10,728	171,046	6,365
Long-term liabilities					1,279,845	
Deferred revenues	9,416	24,174	746	16,255	50,591	
Total liabilities	23,162	29,312	788	26,983	1,501,482	6,365
Total retained earnings/fund balances	92,155	47,281	81,410	69,017	831,036	7,500
Total equity and other credits	92,155	47,281	81,140	69,017	2,453,346	7,500
Total liabilities, equity and other credits	$115,317	$76,593	$82,198	$96,000	$3,954,828	$13,865

Source: City of Charlotte documents.

Exhibit 7.8 City of Charlotte, North Carolina: Combined Statement of Revenues, Expenditures, and Charges in Fund Balances All Government Fund Types and Discretely Presented Component Unit for the Year Ended June 30, 1998 (in thousands)

REVENUES:	General	Special Revenue	Debt Service	Capital Projects	Totals (Memorandum Only) Primary Government	Auditorium-Coliseum-Convention Center Authority Component Unit	Totals (Memorandum Only) Reporting Entity
Property taxes	$150,331	$3,605	$25,137	$5,227	$184,300	$	$184,300
Other taxes	33,044	18,082	11,160		62,286		62,286
Intergovernmental	56,711	25,126	3,649	225	85,711		85,711
Licenses, permits, and fees	21,122		38		21,160		21,160
Interest on investments	5,323	3,205	3,269	3,220	15,017	468	15,485
Administrative charges	9,014				9,014		9,014
Charges for current services	2,874				2,874	13,099	15,973
Fines, forfeitures, and penalties	1,893				1,893		1,893
Facility fees		1,630			1,630	7,940	9,570
Storm water fees		13,846			13,846		13,846
Other	4,224	3,183	585	317	8,309	1,518	9,827
Total revenues	284,536	68,677	43,838	8,989	406,040	23,025	429,065
EXPENDITURES:							
Current							
Public safety	154,738				154,738		154,738
Environmental health and sanitation	27,952	7,417			35,369		35,369
General administration	20,442	3,908			24,350	7,370	31,720
Support services	7,571				7,571		7,571
Engineering and property management	14,321				14,321		14,321
Streets and highways	9,437	14,602			24,039		24,039
Culture and recreation						15,566	15,566

(Continued)

Exhibit 7.8 Continued

REVENUES:	General	Special Revenue	Debt Service	Capital Projects	Totals (Memorandum Only) Primary Government	Auditorium-Coliseum-Convention Center Authority Component Unit	Totals (Memorandum Only) Reporting Entity
Community planning and development	8,637	14,803			23,440		3,440
Job development		2,742			2,742		2,742
Capital outlay				53,849	53,849		53,849
Debt service							
Principal retirement			34,053		34,053		34,053
Interest, fees and other			26,940		26,940		26,940
Total expenditures	243,098	43,472	60,993	53,849	401,412	22,936	424,348
Revenues over (under) expenditures	41,438	25,205	-17,155	-44,860	4,628	89	4,717
OTHER FINANCING SOURCES (USES):							
Total other financing sources (uses)	-31,320	-29,571	33,126	38,548	10,783	190	10,973
Revenues and other sources over (under) expenditures and other uses	10,118	-4,366	15,971	-6,312	15,411	279	15,690
FUND BALANCES, beginning of year	82,037	51,647	65,439	75,329	274,452	7,221	281,673
FUND BALANCES, end of year	$92,155	$47,281	$81,410	$69,017	$289,863	$7,500	$297,363

Source: City of Charlotte documents.

Exhibit 7.9   Timeline for Charlotte and Its Arenas

Year	Activity
1950	Charlotte's first, Independence Arena, built to hold 11,000 people and the Authority established.
1975	Business and political leaders discuss a new coliseum to hold ACC games.
1981	Bond referendum for new coliseum is defeated.
1983	Committee of 100 recommends an uptown arena be built for ACC games; plan abandoned.
1984	With a suburban location, voter referendum passes.
1987	Hornets NBA franchise awarded to George Shinn of Charlotte, North Carolina.
1987	Coliseum design modified to better accommodate professional basketball—23,000 seats plus 12 suites, the Hive becomes reality.
1988	The Hive opens in time for Hornets' inaugural season; rent is $1/game. Council votes to maintain Independence Arena for Charlotte Checkers (hockey team).
1990	Lease renegotiation for Hornets. Shinn indicates he may have to move the team; rent is $7,000 to $9,000 per game.
1996	City manager-appointed Cameron Committee recommends a new arena for uptown, public polls indicate lack of support for another new arena, committee dissolved.
1998	City Council appoints 15-member citizen New Arena Committee.
1999	First report by New Arena Committee due to council by December 1999: Reaction to the Cameron Committee recommendation.
2000	Second report due July 1: location, budget, and size/design recommendations. Final report due December: location, financing, final design.

❖ FIRST COLISEUM BUILT IN 1950—OUTGROWN

The city's original coliseum, built in 1950, only held 11,000 people—not large enough to host events such as the Atlantic Coast Conference (ACC) basketball finals or touring concerts. In 1975, Charlotte political and business leaders began to discuss the need for a new coliseum. The mayor and the coliseum manager proposed public funding for a new coliseum; however, the voters defeated a public bond referendum for $4 million to buy land in 1981. According to the *Charlotte Observer,* the defeat was because the proposal was "vague." Citizens might have supported a more specific proposal with more definitive information about the location and purpose of the coliseum (see Exhibit 7.9 for a summary timeline for Charlotte and its arenas).

In 1983, in an effort to strengthen support, Mayor Eddie Knox appointed a "Committee of 100," so named because of the 100 civic and business leaders that served on it to review sites for a new coliseum. That the mayor appointed the committee reflected the near unanimity among local business and political leaders that a new 25,000-seat coliseum was needed in Charlotte to bolster its image as a dynamic, progressive city. The only issue that really needed attention was where to locate the coliseum to garner sufficient voter approval for a bond referendum to finance the facility. An uptown location was considered to be a cornerstone of urban redevelopment. A survey was conducted through local restaurants and shopping centers to not only capture Charlotte citizen input, but that of visitors as well.

Much to the consternation of uptown business leaders interested in accessibility and status for the City of Charlotte, the citizen survey revealed strong support for a suburban location. Based on the citizen survey results, the "Committee of 100" favored a suburban location for the Hive in their recommendation, although many business and political leaders continued to lean toward an uptown site. Business and civic leaders voiced support for locating the Hive uptown because the street system was already there to handle large numbers of vehicles, and game-day traffic would not normally conflict with business rush hours; restaurants and hotels were already in place to accommodate visitors; and parking was already available, and the city would benefit from parking revenues. Costs, however, were estimated to be substantially higher for an uptown site rather than a suburban location because of the higher land values.

Because of the tension between the results of a citizen survey for a suburban location and continuing civic leadership support for an uptown site, the public referendum was delayed and a national consultant was hired by the city council to study the two options. As many civic leaders had hoped, the consultant's report recommended an uptown site connected to the civic center and to include a hotel, restaurants, and other commercial activity. However, the selected site was too small to accommodate the extent of commercial development and therefore increased the public cost of the project. Eventually, the plan was abandoned.

In 1983, a newly elected mayor, Harvey Gantt, continued to pursue uptown sites for a new arena. In response, the city council contracted with a local consulting firm that developed a proposal requiring a relatively complex financing strategy (40% public contribution) that would also have delayed actual construction of the facility by almost a year. With a November 1984 bond referendum vote looming, the city council voted for the faster, totally publicly funded option of locating a new coliseum on the suburban site. "The City Council ultimately had to decide between two different scenarios: provide the community with a relatively inexpensive facility that satisfied the greatest portion of the city's capital growth needs or ensure a palatable voter referendum by quickly constructing a facility which could compete for the regional entertainment dollar" (Marvin, p. 12). In November 1984, 57% of the voters approved $63.4 million in 25-year revenue bonds over ten years for a suburban coliseum.

The new Charlotte Coliseum was designed to be an all-purpose community facility fully capable of housing major college basketball events. During construction, the prospects of an NBA franchise arose and additional amenities were incorporated once the NBA franchise was secured. The old coliseum was maintained for smaller venues, renamed Independence Arena, and became the home of the Charlotte Checkers minor league hockey team.

❖ THE NBA—BIG-CITY STATUS FOR CHARLOTTE

George Shinn, a relatively unknown owner of a number of for-profit business training schools, wanted to bring major league baseball to Charlotte; but the chances for an expansion team were remote. The NBA, however, was in an expansion mode in 1986. Charlotte was rated least likely of the seven teams that paid the $100,000 application fee to be awarded a franchise.

NBA Expansion

The NBA, which began in 1946 with eleven teams, added expansion teams as owners voted to add them. The commissioner of the league in 1986, David Stern, strongly supported growth of the league. The NBA shared national broadcast revenues as well as licensed product revenues with all teams in the league. Other team revenues, such as gate receipts, local broadcast revenues, and arena revenues were totally for the benefit of the individual team.

Shinn, with the help of a local sports marketing consultant, put together a presentation to overcome the lack of knowledge about Charlotte and the region as well as the perception that it was only a "college" basketball town. The city's citizens rallied behind the idea of professional basketball. Shinn sold more than 15,000 season tickets (with a large deposit required and without a team). The new coliseum was nearly completed, and Shinn negotiated a $1 per game lease for the first five years. Charlotte, to the surprise of many, was the first NBA expansion team named. Shinn paid $32.5 million for the Hornets franchise that was awarded in April 1987 to begin play during the 1988–1989 season. The new Charlotte Hive was completed in the summer of 1988 and ready for the inaugural season. The Hive had 23,500 seats for basketball (22,919 were revenue producing) with twelve skyboxes (suites). A parade was held to honor Shinn.

The Hornets' Success

The success of the Hornets in the early years far surpassed both Shinn's and the city's most optimistic projections. Benefiting from the $1 per game coliseum rental and the NBA salary cap, the Hornets' revenues exceeded expenses by nearly $4 million in its first year. The average NBA team could expect to earn 60% of its revenue through ticket sales and the remainder from the franchise's share of league licensing of broadcast advertising sponsorship rights.

For its first eight years, the team's play was not stellar, but the Hornets had enough victories to keep the fans hopeful. Despite the team's poor performance, season tickets and the few individual game tickets available consistently sold out and the Charlotte Hornets had the highest number of tickets sold of any of the teams in the league. When it was time to renegotiate the lease in 1990, the love affair with Shinn began to fade. He insisted that if he did not receive a favorable lease, he would move the team. Several print and broadcast commentators and talk show hosts opined that Shinn needed a publicist to rein in his mouth or better yet speak for him and that Shinn needed to learn to negotiate instead of demand. An agreement was finally reached (the "Revised Agreement") for the Hornets to pay rent of $7,000 to $9,000 per game plus expenses with the team receiving all of the courtside advertising dollars generated (previously the team received 50% of the courtside advertising dollars).

❖ NBA SPORTS EQUALS NBA ENTERTAINMENT

In the 1990s, the NBA/entertainment world became more demanding in terms of the requirements placed on potential host facilities. It was

Exhibit 7.10   Hornets Revenue Growth Compared to Expenses
Growth, 1992–1998

	Percent of Growth in Revenues	Percent of Growth in Operating Expenses	Percent of Growth in Player Salaries and Benefits
Fiscal Year 1992–1993	100%	100%	100%
Fiscal Year 1993–1994	107	127	138
Fiscal Year 1994–1995	117	130	135
Fiscal Year 1995–1996	128	176	174*
Fiscal Year 1996–1997	132	148	147
Fiscal Year 1997–1998	157	182	192

* Percentage relationship skewed higher because of accounting principle requiring recording of all future payments to the New York Knicks for the trade of Larry Johnson as an expense.

Source: Charlotte Hornets based on annual audited financial statements.

becoming increasingly apparent that the Hive was not able to meet the needs of the Hornets franchise or many other events that Charlotte hoped to host there. Although most professional teams' revenues were increasing, expenses were increasing at a faster rate driven by escalating player salaries (see Exhibit 7.10).

Arena Suites—An Important Revenue Stream

By 1996, when Shinn was considering relocating the Hornets, eight NBA teams were relative "have nots" because they received substantially less revenue than those teams with arenas that had private suites. The "have nots" included:

Orlando Magic   Atlanta Hawks
Dallas Mavericks   Houston Rockets
Charlotte Hornets   Los Angeles Clippers
Miami Heat   Los Angeles Lakers

According to Revenues from Sports Venues, suite prices for NBA teams vary from a low of $83,000 to a high of $147,585 per suite, per season. In 1996, five arenas had no private suites. Of those arenas that did have private suites, Charlotte had the fewest with 12 and the United Center in Chicago the most with 216 (see Exhibit 7.11 for private suites in NBA facilities). The average number of suites across the NBA

Exhibit 7.11   NBA Arenas

Team	Arena	Location	Year Built	Other Tenant	Percent Public Ownership	Capacity	No. Suites	Club Seats
Atlanta Hawks	Phillips Arena	D	1999	NHL (Thrashers)	30	20,000	96	2,983
Boston Celtics	Fleet Center	D	1995	NHL (Bruins)	0	19,600	104	2,350
Charlotte Hornets	Charlotte Coliseum†	N	1988		100	23,698	12	0
Chicago Bulls	United Center	O	1994	NHL (Blackhawks)	7	21,500	216	3,300
Cleveland Cavaliers	Gund Arena	D	1994	AHL (Lumberjacks)	100	20,500	88	2,050
Dallas Mavericks	American Airlines Center	D	2001*	NHL (Stars)	36	20,000*	120*	1,800
Denver Nuggets	Pepsi Center	D	1999	NHL (Avalanche)	3	19,300	95	1,854*
Detroit Pistons	Palace of Auburn Hills	N	1988	IHL (Vipers)	0	21,454	180	1,000
Golden State Warriors	Arena in Oakland	N	1966/1997		100	19,200	72	3,550
Houston Rockets	Compaq Center†	N	1975		100	16,611	16	0
Indiana Pacers	Conseco Fieldhouse*	D	1999	IHL (Ice)	51	18,500*	69	2,522
LA Clippers	Staples Center*	D	1999	NHL (Kings)	19	19,282	160	2,500*
LA Lakers	Staples Center*	D	1999	NHL (Kings)	19	20,000*	160	2,500*
Miami Heat	American Airlines Arena	D	1999	NHL (Panthers)	49	19,000*	156	302*
Milwaukee Bucks	Bradley Center	D	1988	AHL (Admirals)	0	18,633	67	0
Minnesota Timberwolves	Target Center	D	1990/1995		19	19,006	68	0
New Jersey Nets	Continental Airlines Arena†	N	1981	NHL (Devils)	100	20,039	29	0
New York Knicks	Madison Square Garden	D	1968/1991	NHL (Rangers)	50	20,700	89	2,600

Team	Arena	Location	Year Built	Other Tenant	Percent Public Ownership	Capacity	No. Suites	Club Seats
Orlando Magic	Orlando Arena	D	1989	IHL (Solar Bears)	100	17,248	22	0
Philadelphia 76ers	First Union Center	O	1996	NHL (Flyers)	11	19,253	126	2,065
Phoenix Suns	America West Arena	D	1992	NHL (Coyotes)	47	19,100	88	3,108
Portland Trailblazers	Rose Garden	D	1995		13	21,500	70	1,744
Sacramento Kings	ARCO Arena	N	1988		50	17,317	30	442
San Antonio Spurs	Alamodome†	D	1993		100	20,500	32	3,172
Seattle SuperSonics	Key Arena	O	1962/1995		9	17,100	58	1,060
Toronto Raptors	Air Canada Centre	D	1999	NHL (Maple Leafs)	0	22,500	140	5,000
Utah Jazz	Delta Center	D	1991		21	19,911	56	0
Vancouver Grizzlies	General Motors Place	D	1995	NHL (Canucks)	0	19,100	92	2,398
Washington Wizzards	MCI Center	D	1997	NHL (Capitals)	22	19,608	110	2,983
				Average existing arena		19,086	72	2,367
				Average new arena		20,133	104	1,976

* Currently under construction.
† Considering new arena in 2001.
Source: NBA, *Charlotte Observer*, telephone interviews.

in January 1999 was 72. The overall average revenue for the arenas with private suites was $2.8 million. The Hornets had $925,000 in revenue from private suites (tickets had to be purchased separately).

By 1999, six of the "have not" teams had new arenas under construction. Only the Orlando Magic and Charlotte Hornets did not have specific sites being developed. The majority of the new arenas were being built in downtown areas on approximately five acres. In addition to basketball, most expected to house other sports teams such as hockey, arena football, indoor soccer, or indoor lacrosse.

❖   A NEW ARENA PROPOSED

In 1996, the city manager—without the city council's involvement— appointed the "Cameron Committee" (informally named after C. C. Cameron, a retired First Union CEO who chaired it). City Manager Wendell White selected eleven of the most influential community leaders in Charlotte and charged them to explore alternative ways to meet the long-term facility requirements of the Charlotte Hornets. The Committee identified four options: (a) do nothing, (b) renegotiate the Hornets' lease and renovate the Hive at a cost of $7 million, (c) sell the Hive to the Hornets, or (d) provide direct or indirect assistance with the development of a new arena. The committee recommended the fourth option because they wanted the Hornets to share the costs as well as the benefits and they wanted the city to retain control of the new arena for scheduling non-Hornets events.

In November 1996, uptown business interests entered into the process and presented their financing proposal. The Cameron Committee plan included a $192 million arena/entertainment/retail complex in Uptown Charlotte. The Cameron Committee would have the Hornets pay $109 million of the cost of a new arena of which $59 million was expected from the sale of luxury suites, club seats, and other promotions. The public would pay $58 million of the new arena's cost, and the remaining $25 million to build the entertainment/retail complex would come from local Charlotte companies. The council agreed not to raise property taxes to build the facility. Supporters of the arena suggested that funds be raised by imposing seat taxes, increasing the uptown district tax (the uptown area is a special service area with a higher tax rate than other districts to fund redevelopment projects within the center city area), or using proceeds from the sale of the old convention center. If only the arena were constructed, the scaled-down cost was expected to be $155 million and the City of Charlotte would be asked to pay $46 million. The plan was totally unacceptable to the Hornets from a financial standpoint. Shinn did not want to commit even $50 million of his capital in a project controlled by the city.

Through a variety of avenues, the public expressed its outrage that there was little citizen input to the Cameron Committee plan. A poll of local citizens found that 75% of the public responding said they did not want government to build a new arena. There were groups including the Black Political Caucus, the Citizens for Effective Government, the League of Women Voters, and the Chamber of Citizens that were furious that the city would build an arena for basketball teams because Charlotte already had the Hive for basketball. The public demanded that no public dollars be spent on another coliseum when "we had a perfectly good one," and tax dollars were needed for other things such as schools and fighting crime. The entire process became even more muddled by events surrounding the owner, Shinn.

Owner Troubles

The Hornets fans slowly began to feel disenfranchised because of a succession of events: the first coach, Allan Bristow, was fired in his third year; highly drafted players did not pan out; a key player (Larry Johnson) was given an $84 million contract and then was injured and eventually traded; other key players were allowed to leave as free agents; and on and on. Because Shinn kept tight control and did not allow others to make these important player decisions, the public through letters to the editor, sports talk shows, and news commentators blamed him for the lackluster performance of the Hornets.

Then in September 1997, a woman alleged that Shinn forced sexual relations with her at his home just across the state border in South Carolina. The South Carolina prosecutor decided not to prosecute the case, although he thought there was probable cause that a crime was committed, but not enough evidence to convince a jury "beyond a reasonable doubt." Later, the prosecutor decided to reopen and expand the sexual assault charges against Shinn, because he discovered that the South Carolina Law Enforcement Division's lead agent on the 1997 case had been ordered by her boss not to check leads about other possible assault accusations against Shinn. In a civil suit brought by Shinn's original accuser, two other women testified that he had also forced them to engage in sexual activity.

These personal problems, covered extensively in the news media, and Shinn's involvement in the team hiring and firing decisions, also covered in the media, led to speculation that Shinn himself would be the reason that the public would not support spending the public's tax dollars on a new arena. When Michael Jordan (a North Carolina native, graduate of the University of North Carolina, and three-time winner of the MVP award in the NBA) was involved with discussions about a partnership with Shinn, the prospects for a new arena improved. However, Shinn would not agree to 50% involvement by Jordan in either team management or financial management and discussions were terminated.

A New Charlotte Arena Proposed—Again

In the summer of 1998, because Shinn stated that he would have to move the franchise, the city council and Mayor Patrick McCrory reengaged the process yet another time by appointing an advisory committee of fifteen members. This time, each member of the city council appointed one member to the New Arena Committee and the mayor appointed four members, one of whom served as the chair (see Exhibit 7.12 for members of the New Arena Committee and who appointed them).

The New Arena Committee was charged to do the following:

- Review and confirm previous recommendations regarding the need for a new facility—including size, location, and cost—and report to the city council its recommendations on or before January 1, 1999.
- Develop one or more models for the council's consideration that included funding, financing, ownership, etc., and present such models to the city council on or before July 1, 1999.
- Make recommendations to the city council concerning public involvement in the new arena process on or before December 31, 1999.

The city council would make the final decision on which—if any—of the New Arena Committee recommendations to accept. A simple

Exhibit 7.12   New Arena Committee

Name	Occupation	Appointed by
Mahlon Adams	Real estate broker	Sara Spencer, District 1
Frank Barnes	Professor, University of North Carolina Charlotte	Don Reid, at-large
David Chadwick	Pastor, Forest Hills Presbyterian Church	Pat McCrory, mayor
William C. Covington	Retired banker	Pat McCrory, mayor
Eric Douglas	Boy Scouts of America	Malachi Greene, District 2
John Fennebresque, chair	Attorney, Fennebresque, Clark, Swindell & Hay	Pat McCrory, mayor
Anthony Fox	Attorney, Parker Poe Adams and Bernstein	Pat McCrory, mayor
Gerald Johnson	Publisher, Charlotte Post	Nasif Majeed, District 4
Ray Kennedy	American Products Distribution	Patrick Cannon, District 3
John Maxhiem	Chairman/CEO, Piedmont Natural Gas Company	Rod Autrey, at-large
Sam Smith	Tryon Systems Corporation	Al Rousso, at-large
Stan Vaughn	Coopers & Lybrand (CPAs)	Charles Baker, District 6
Alan Wells	Gordon Wells Company	Tim Sellers, District 5
Ed Woodall	Dent Demon	Mike Jackson, District 7
Ron Wooten	First Union	Lynn Wheeler, at-large

majority of the council was sufficient to adopt a recommendation; however, the mayor did not have a vote unless there was a tie among the city councilmembers.

Plan to Move the Team on Hold
Awaiting an Authority/Hornets Agreement

The appointment of the New Arena Committee was the first step in yet another attempt to reach a new agreement between the Authority and the Charlotte Hornets (see Exhibit 7.13 for a summary of the Authority/Hornets agreements over time). At the outset, all of the parties were on record in their desire that the Hornets remain in Charlotte. The city council recognized that there was an economic impact from having a professional basketball team. In a study commissioned by the Hornets, a UNC Charlotte professor estimated that annually more than $100 million of revenue—not recoverable from other sources—would be lost to the city's economy if the team were to leave.[1] In addition, the council recognized the current trend with respect to state-of-the-art basketball arenas for NBA franchises to be competitive. To this end, the parties expressed a commitment to

Exhibit 7.13   Summary of Coliseum Authority Lease Agreements
With the Charlotte Hornets Over Time

Description	Original Agreement	Revised Agreement	New Agreement	Amended Agreement
Effective Date	Oct. 1, 1988	Oct. 1, 1992	Nov. 5, 1995	April 13, 1998
Term	5 years	5 years	5 years	6 years
Renewal Term	5 years	5 years	5 years	1 year (twice)
Notice	None	None	3 years	90 days*
Termination	None	None	$250,000 in Year 5	$30 million in 1999 or 2000, $20 million in 2001, $10 million in 2002 or 2003
Ticket Revenue	Retained by team	Retained by team	Retained by team	Retained by team
Rent	$1.00/game	$7,000 to 9,000/game	$9,000/game	$9,000/game
Event Expenses	Paid by team	Paid by team	Paid by team	Paid by team
Novelties	100% to team	100% to team	100% to team	100% to team
Advertising	50% to team	100% courtside, 50% permanent to team	100% courtside, 50% permanent to team	100% courtside, 50% permanent to team, naming rights†
Food and Beverage	0% to team	0% to team	50% profit to team	50% profit to team
Parking	0% to team	0% to team	50% profit to team	50% profit to team
Other Franchises	With team's permission	With team's permission	Allowed	Allowed
Additional Revenues	n/a	$1.0 million	$1.5 million	20% of 1st $2 million excess funds, 80% over $2 million

* If the Hornets do not sell more than 15,750 per game average or if the New Coliseum
   Committee does not meet the deadlines established in the Amended Agreement.
† The Hornets receive the first $400,000 and the city participates after that is reached.
Source: Compiled from City of Charlotte documents.

negotiate mutually satisfactory terms of a new agreement that would
result in the Hornets making a long-term commitment to the new arena.

The term of the new agreement was from July 1, 1998, to July 1,
2004, although the Hornets could withdraw from the agreement by

Total Revenues and Expenses	Coliseum Total	Attributable to Hornets	Attributable to Other Events	Hornets Percentage of Total
Operating Revenues	$122,922,957	$64,065,508	$58,857,449	52.12%
Operating Expenses	85,983,707	47,682,157	42,640,208	55.45
Operating Surplus (Deficit)	36,939,250	20,721,99	616,217,241	56.10
Revenue Sharing	4,338,645	4,338,645		100.00
Surplus Net of Revenue Sharing	32,600,605	16,383,351	16,217,241	50.25

Exhibit 7.14   Revenues and Expenses Attributable to the Charlotte Hornets Fiscal 1989–1999

paying a $250,000 penalty. The initial understanding for the new agreement gave the Hornets the benefit of additional Hive revenue, but it did not jeopardize the city's day-to-day control of the Hive or the Authority's ability to meet its current financial responsibilities. What the new agreement really provided was an opportunity for more time to revisit the issue of the extent of public participation in the financing of a new arena. Financially, the team would receive a portion of bottom-line profits generated by the Hive, the Hornets gained the right to namė the Hive and would benefit from the first dollars generated by the naming rights agreement. (The NFL Carolina Panthers football team sold the right to name the stadium "Ericsson Stadium" for ten years at $20 million.) In the Hornets' agreement, the Authority and the city would benefit from any naming rights revenue in excess of $400,000 annually. Hornets-promoted events held in the Hive, including Hornets home games, would continue to pay rent. The agreement was to benefit the Hornets and the Authority, both of which recognized that the Hornets made a substantial contribution to the Hive's operating surplus (see Exhibits 7.14 and 7.15).

The managing director of the Authority said a Policy Committee would oversee the operation of the Hive. The committee was made up of two representatives of the Hornets organization, two representatives of the Authority, and one representative of the city manager's office. The agreement offered the Hornets additional space in the Hive, specifically the advance ticket office facility, use of the Hive's conference room, and free rent for Hornets-related free, charitable, and community-related events. If all of the parties involved in this agreement lived

---

Exhibit 7.15   Review of Use of Coliseum Operating Surpluses

Total Coliseum Operating Surpluses, Fiscal 1989 to 1998	$32,600,605
Average Surplus Fiscal 1989–1995	$3,665,230
Average Surplus Fiscal 1996–1997	$2,314,664
Use of Coliseum Operating Surpluses	
Charlotte Coliseum Capital Projects	10,291,108
Ovens Auditorium/Independence Arena Capital Projects	7,785,540
Old Charlotte Convention Center Capital Projects	1,680,628
New Charlotte Convention Center Capital Projects	2,598,724
Old Convention Center Operating Deficits	1,225,695
New Charlotte Convention Center Operating Deficits	2,352,078
Increase in Authority Operating Funds	4,466,832
Net Proceeds Committed to Debt Service Fund	2,200,000
Total	$32,600,605

Source: City of Charlotte documents.

---

up to their obligations and the decision to build a new arena were to go forward, there would be a 31-year partnership between the Hornets and the City of Charlotte.

However, in the event that the team, the Authority, or the city failed to live up to its part of the bargain, there were several remedies in place for the affected parties to terminate the agreement. The city was protected in that if the Hornets were to leave Charlotte at any time during the life of the new agreement, they could do so by paying the city an amount of money roughly equal to the outstanding debt service on the to-be-constructed new arena (the amount would be dependent on when the agreement might be terminated). The Hornets were protected in that if the city failed to make progress toward a decision on whether or not to build a new arena, the team could terminate the contract. Both parties were also protected by the season-ticket sales clause: if season ticket sales fell below 15,750 after July 1, 2001, the agreement could be terminated. If the city committed to building a new facility and successfully negotiated a lease or use agreement for that facility with the Hornets and season ticket sales held up, the Hornets were obligated to play in the Hive until the new arena was opened and for an extended term in the new facility. The agreement called for the community to make a final decision concerning public participation in a new arena by December 31, 2000. If the December 2000 deadline was not met, the contract could be altered by the Hornets to conclude in 2001 (rather than 2004).

❖ ARENAS ACROSS THE NATION
FINANCED IN DIFFERENT WAYS

The four major professional sports leagues—the NBA, Major League Baseball (MLB), the National Football League (NFL), and the National Hockey League (NHL)—had 105 teams in 24 states in the United States and Canada. Because several teams shared facilities, there were 83 stadiums/arenas in operation in 1999. During the most recent decades, 16 new stadiums were built in the 1960s, 20 in the 1970s, and 13 in the 1980s; however, in the 1990s, 41 new arenas (or major renovations) were completed, or were about to be completed by 2000 or were planned for construction. The explosion of new stadiums reflected the increasing importance of the revenue generated from the facility where the team played (Rafool, 1997).

The more profitable the facility was expected to be, the less demand there was for public participation in the construction. When baseball accounted for all or most of the professional teams playing in stadiums, private sources accounted for the financing of all stadiums. As other professional sports emerged, building stadiums became viewed as public works because of the enormous cost of building the larger facilities, especially for football. During the 1960s and 1970s, most stadiums were constructed with public dollars and private financing was the exception. By the 1980s, a combination of public and private financing was common; the facility built entirely with public funds, such as Charlotte's Hive, became the exception. In the 1990s, there was still heavy reliance on public financing for sports arenas; however, it became far more common to have shared public and private financing of the projects. Owners of sports franchises were more willing to spend millions of dollars for new stadiums when two teams occupied the same facility because of the opportunities for additional revenues.

A number of joint public/private financing methods emerged. Public sources of revenue included the levying of taxes, issuance of bonds by a city, contributions of land, and the appropriation of general funds or grants. Private sources included arena revenues (club seats, suites), naming rights, club contributions, as well as concessions and parking (see Exhibit 7.16 for examples of public sources of revenues).

The primary vehicle for generating public financing was bonds. Bonds could be issued by a state, city, county, or special authority;

Exhibit 7.16   Potential Sources of Public Funds and Methods of
Financing—Existing Arenas

Potential Sources of Funds and Vehicles Used	Sources	Facility	Year Built
City Sales Tax			
City of Los Angeles	General sales tax	Staples Center	1999
*County Sales Tax**			
Lodging tax			
City of Phoenix	Hotel/motel	America West Arena	1992
City of Dallas	Hotel/motel	New Dallas Arena	2001
Excise tax (alcohol, cigarettes, gas, etc.)			
City of Phoenix	Excise taxes	America West Arena	1992
City Portland	Gasoline tax	Rose Garden	1995
Property Tax			
City of Salt Lake City	Tax increment financing funds	Delta Center	1991
Metro. Comm. Develop. Authority	Tax increment financing funds	Target Center	1990
City of Dallas	Tax increment financing funds	New Dallas Arena	2001
Prof. Sports Develop. Area	Tax increment financing funds	Conseco Fieldhouse	1999
City of Los Angeles	Property tax	Staples Center	1999
*Lottery Funds/Gaming**			
Admission, Concession, Parking Taxes			
City of Portland	6% city user fee	Rose Garden	1995
City of Los Angeles	City parking tax	Staples Center	1999
City of Los Angeles	5% city ticket tax	Staples Center	1999
Contribution of Land			
District of Columbia	Land purchase and contribution	MCI Center	1997
United Center	Land contribution	United Center	1994
Dade County	Land contribution	American Airlines Arena	1999
City of Los Angeles	Land purchase and contribution	Staples Center	1999
State Grants, Rebates, or Contributions			
State of Pennsylvania	Grant	First Union Center	1996
State of Illinois	Grant	United Center	1994
State of Florida	Sales tax rebate	American Airlines Arena	1999
State of Indiana	Infrastructure grant	Conseco Fieldhouse	1999

Potential Sources of Funds and Vehicles Used	Sources	Facility	Year Built
County Contribution			
Dade County	Operating Subsidy	American Airlines Arena	1999
City Contribution			
City of Philadelphia	Miscellaneous debt	First Union Center	1996
City of Phoenix	General fund revenue/invest. income	America West Arena	1992
City of Seattle	Capital/operating funds, interest earnings	Key Arena	1995
City of Chicago	Infrastructure improvements	United Center	1994
City of Indianapolis	City investment income	Conseco Fieldhouse	1999
Federal Grants			
City of Minneapolis	Parking facility acquisition	Target Center	1990
Business Fees/Licenses			
City of Los Angeles	Business license fees	Staples Center	1999
Other			
City of Los Angeles	Utilities taxes	Staples Center	1999
District of Columbia	Special district arena tax	MCI Center	1997
Prof. sports develop. area	Captured state sales/income taxes	Conseco Fieldhouse	1999
Financing Vehicles Used			
Revenue Bonds			
City of Portland	6% user fee, gasoline tax	Rose Garden	1995
City of Phoenix	Excise, hotel/motel, car rental taxes	America West Arena	1992
Atlanta-Fulton County Authority	Auto rental tax, arena revenues	Philips Arena	1999
District of Columbia	Special district arena tax	MCI Center	1997
City of Seattle	Arena revenues, general fund	Key Arena	1995
City of Los Angeles	City sales, excise and misc. taxes	Staples Center	1999
City of Dallas	Hotel/motel, car rental, lease revenues	New Dallas Arena	2001
City of Oakland-Alameda County	Arena revenues, city/county sources	New Oakland Arena	1997
Metro Community Develop. Authority	Tax increment financing funds, entertainment tax, parking revenues	Target Center	1990

(Continued)

Exhibit 7.16 Continued

Potential Sources of Funds and Vehicles Used	Sources	Facility	Year Built
G.O. Bonds			
City of Seattle	Arena revenues, general fund	Key Arena	1995
City of Dallas	General funds	New Dallas Arena	2001
City of Minneapolis	Tax increment financing funds, entertainment tax, parking revenues	Target Center	1990
*Certificates of Participation**			
Tax Increment Financing†			
City of Salt Lake City	Property taxes	Delta Center	1991
Metro Community Develop. Authority	Property taxes	Target Center	1990
City of Dallas	Property taxes	New Dallas Arena	2001
Prof. Sports Develop. Area	Property taxes	Conseco Fieldhouse	1999
Bank Financing			
Portland Trail Blazers	Arena revenues	Rose Garden	1995
Boston Bruins	Arena revenues	Fleet Center	1995
Phoenix Suns	Arena revenues	America West Arena	1992
Utah Jazz	Arena revenues	Delta Center	1991
Washington Wizards/Capitals	Arena revenues	MCI Center	1997
Minnesota Timberwolves	Arena revenues	Target Center	1990
Chicago Bulls/Blackhawks	Arena revenues	United Center	1994
Los Angeles Kings	Arena revenues	Staples Center	1999
Toronto Raptors/Maple Leafs	Arena revenues	Air Canada Centre	1999
Private Placement			
Dallas Mavericks/Stars	Arena revenues	New Dallas Arena	2001
Portland Trail Blazers	Arena revenues	Rose Garden	1995
Philadelphia 76ers/Flyers	Arena revenues	First Union Center	1996
Miami Heat	Arena revenues	American Airlines Arena	1999

Source: New Arena Committee document.
* Option not used.
† Cannot be used in Charlotte.

however, the amount and use of bonds was restricted by legal limits on the amount of debt the governmental entity could have. In North Carolina, municipalities were restricted to a debt limit not to exceed 8% of the total assessed value of real property within their jurisdiction (see Exhibit 7.17). In 1998, Charlotte's total net outstanding debt was

The Edifice Complex   139

Exhibit 7.17   City of Charlotte Legal Debt Margin—June 30, 1998 (in thousands)

Assessed property value
(100% assessment)..$35,049,255

Gross limitation—8% of assessed property value..$2,803,940

Total outstanding general obligation bonded debt	$774,195	
Amounts due under certificates of participation and other financing agreements primarily for Convention Center, capital improvements and equipment	239,868	
Bonds authorized but unissued	270,455	$1,284,518
Less—water general obligation bonds	254,887	

Outstanding debt, net...$1,029,631

Net legal debt margin..$1,774,309

Source: City of Charlotte documents.

Exhibit 7.18   Ratio of Net General Obligation Bonded Debt to Assessed Value and Net General Obligation Bonded Debt Per Capita for City of Charlotte (Last Ten Fiscal Years in Thousands)

Fiscal Year	Net Bonded Debt	Ratio of Net Bonded Debt to Assessed Value	Net Bonded Debt per Capita
1989	$220.086	1.25%	$562.07
1990	207,868	1.08	525.01
1991	254,550	1.29	635.89
1992	270,901	1.06	641.96
1993	281,523	1.10	654.05
1994	314,908	1.16	709.87
1995	298,373	1.04	655.24
1996	319,653	1.08	686.11
1997	299,918	0.95	637.37
1998	278,630	0.79	548.97

Source: City of Charlotte documents.

---

slightly more than $1 billion; its bonded debt limit was more than $2.8 billion (see Exhibit 7.18). Based on its conservative use of bonded debt management, Charlotte received the best bond ratings of Aaa/AAA that in 1999 resulted in interest rates in the range of between 4.8 and 5.3%.

Bonds could be either general obligation bonds backed by the full faith and credit of the governmental entity issuing the bonds, or they could be revenue bonds supported by a specific revenue stream dedicated to paying off the bond. General obligation bonds required voter approval before they could be issued. Revenue bonds were frequently used to finance sports facilities because the stadium revenues could be used to pay the debt. Revenue bonds did not require a public vote for approval. Tax-exempt revenue bonds that carried the lower interest rates were restricted when used for private purposes: No more than 10% of private stadium revenues could be used to pay debt service on the bonds.

Several governmental entities created special stadium authorities or districts to build and manage sports facilities as separate entities with bonding authority. Special state authorities were created in states such as Illinois and New Jersey, whereas metropolitan authorities existed in places such as Phoenix, Denver, Indianapolis, and Charlotte. The particular organizational arrangement depended on the specific circumstances in each jurisdiction.

Newer markets were successful in building arenas by selling personal seat licenses (PSLs) and preselling luxury suites. Other states authorized use of special local option taxes (for example, states authorized taxes on hotel and motel stays) or fees (such as ticket surcharges) to service the debt for sports facilities. Finally, tax incentives and tax deferrals were used to entice teams to locate in particular states or localities.

A 1994 study (Baade) of local government investment in sports arenas found that in almost three-fourths of the years for which operating revenue data were available, cities earned more income from sports teams than they paid in operating costs. However, it was also found that the escalating costs of constructing modern facilities made it increasingly unlikely that stadiums would return enough revenue to cover debt service expenditures—especially because construction costs tended to exceed projections by 67%. The sports stadiums' accumulated net present value (ANPV) for 13 of the 14 cases examined in the study was negative, indicating that the investment was not fully returned. Baade concluded that cities needed to cover their capital expenses early on and ensure that operating expenses continued to be covered during the life of the stadium, or they would be net losers in the deal over the long run.

❖ NEW ARENA COMMITTEE IN ACTION

The New Arena Committee began its deliberations within the framework outlined in the Agreement between the City of Charlotte and the
Hornets. The Committee members were fully briefed by an experienced national sports consultant hired to assist in the preparation of
background information and comparative data from arena projects in
other cities. The New Arena Committee confirmed the earlier findings
of the Cameron Committee (see Exhibit 7.19): the Hornets needed a
new facility that included suites and club seats. The July 1, 1999, deadline required that the Committee make recommendations on size and
design, location, and cost ranges.

Exhibit 7.19   First Report of the New Arena Committee

MEMORANDUM

Date:	December 14, 1998
From:	New Arena Committee
To:	Mayor Patrick L. McCrory
	City Council Members
Subject:	Report of the New Arena Committee

On behalf of each of the members of the New Arena Committee (the "Committee"), I am
pleased to submit to you this report addressing the initial charge for the Committee established by the Amending Agreement, dated April 13, 1998, among the Coliseum Authority,
George Shinn, the Charlotte Hornets and the city of Charlotte, as follows: "Review and confirm previous recommendations regarding the <u>need</u> for a new facility, including <u>size, location,
and cost</u>, and report to the City Council its recommendations on or before January 1, 1999."
(emphasis added)

- Recommendation. The Committee reaffirms the Cameron Committee's recommendation[1] that the development of a new arena is the best solution to address
  the long-term needs of the Charlotte Hornets, and, therefore, the needs of the
  City of Charlotte. However, the Committee is not in a position at this point to
  make any recommendations as to size, location and cost.[2]

- Basis for Recommendation. The Committee's recommendation is based on the
  following work to date:

  a) Review of the "Cameron Committee" recommendation to City Council, 24
     Uptown Proposal and other information concerning this issue provided by
     the City staff or members of this Committee;

  b) Briefings from and discussions with Jeff Mullins (member of the Cameron
     Committee), Craig Skiem (consultant/advisor to the Cameron Committee)
     and Jim Nash (arena financing specialist for Bank of America);

(Continued)

Exhibit 7.19 Continued

c)   Site visit to the Charlotte Coliseum. The Committee participated in a walk-
ing tour of the current facility and was given presentations by the Coliseum
Authority, the Hornets and City staff. The present Coliseum although not
one of the new state-of-the-art arenas at present may fill the needs of the
City, but does not fill the long-term needs of the Charlotte Hornets, accord-
ing to their financial needs. These have still not been addressed by this
Committee and will not be addressed until the second phase of the
Committee work after January 1, 1999.

d)   Site visits to three state-of-the-art arenas. At each location, the Committee
participated in an extensive walking tour to include not only the "amenities" such as suites and club seating areas, but working spaces such as the
loading docks, marshaling and staging areas. At each location the
Committee was briefed by and had the opportunity to ask questions of representatives at each arena. The three arenas visited:

Gund Arena, Cleveland, Ohio	Opened 1995
First Union Center, Philadelphia	Opened 1996
MCI Center, Washington, D.C.	Opened 1997

Each arena was unique in its own situation. They did however give each Committee
member a good view of many of the things to look for as we a Ddress the new arena question.
The visit to these arenas made it obvious the real difference between our present Coliseum
and the new entertainment complexes being built since 1994. It also gave each member of the
Committee a feel for the size, cost and complexity for the new generation of sports complexes
that are being built today.

• Size, Location and Cost. Although each of these issues has been discussed generally, the Committee has unanimously agreed that the issues are sufficiently
complex so that no meaningful recommendation may be made to the City
Council at this point. Rather, the Committee has decided to study the details of
each of these issues in three sub-committees, each of which is co-chaired by two
Committee members. The sub-committees' recommendations will be reviewed
by the full Committee and, if acceptable, presented to City Council together
with the Committee's report due July 1, 1999.

• General Comments of the Chairman. Speaking as Chairman of the Committee,
I want to convey to you that I have been very impressed with the thoughtful-
ness and dedication to this arena issue that each of the diverse members of the
Committee has exhibited throughout this process so far. I look forward to working with this Committee as we accomplish the tasks put before us.

---

[1] The Cameron Commission's recommendation was presented to Charlotte City
Council on February 10, 1997. This recommendation also contained a caveat that the
Cameron Commission was unclear, at the time, whether the new arena option
maximized the City's financial position or impacted the existing expenditure plan of
the City. Based on our work to date, the Committee reaffirms this position.
[2] Despite the lack of recommendation in this report as to size, location, cost, we have
attached a letter from the Charolotte Hornets that they are fully satisfied that the
Committe has fulfilled its initial charge per Section 7.4 of the Amending Agreement.
Source: City of Charlotte documents.

Exhibit 7.20   New Arena Requirements as Outlined
by the Charlotte Hornets

1. Capacity

Regular Seats	17,500
Club Seats	2,500
Suite Seats	1,920 (80 suites with 14 seats + 10 tickets each)
Total	21,920 tickets to be sold

2. Mascot, cheerleader, anthem singers, and half-time acts dressing rooms

3. Marketing hospitality rooms (6) to be used simultaneously with capacity of 50–200

4. Office space for team staff (100 employees)

5. Signage: fascia and concourse

6. Built in TV and radio facilities including studios, control rooms, offices, reception, etc.

7. Street access restaurant and bar

8. Team store

9. Interactive area

10. Food court

11. Lots of storage

12. Shop/industrial arts area

13. Museum

14. Archive room

15. Fountain (outside)

16. Ticketing operations area

17. Restrooms

Source: City of Charlotte documents.

Deliberations of the New Arena Subcommittee on Size and Design

The Size and Design Subcommittee asked the Hornets to outline size and space needs for the committee as a place to start (see Exhibit 7.20). The members felt that it was important for the entire committee to visit several facilities of different sizes and locations, to view different configurations, and to talk with people who had experience with the facilities. The entire New Arena Committee visited three different sites: Gund Arena in Cleveland, First Union Center in Philadelphia, and the MCI Center in Washington, DC. A series of questions were asked at each location. The committee felt the trip was valuable in helping them to understand the size and design requirements of the Hornets.

Deliberations of the New Arena Subcommittee on Location

The New Arena Subcommittee on Location agreed on the following selection criteria for a proposed location:

Transportation—highways, transit, parking availability
Environment—compatibility to adjacent uses, hazardous waste, related off-site development
Parcel—size (approximately 5 acres was needed), configuration, number of different owners
Location—demographics, adjacent facilities
Costs—acquisition and infrastructure costs

Fifteen initial sites were identified as meeting the selection criteria. After several weeks of examining the various sites the subcommittee pared the list to just five sites in the uptown area of the city plus the site where the Hive was located (see Exhibit 7.21 for a map that identifies the locations). The five sites were grouped into three general areas: one northeast of Ericsson football stadium; two southeast of the Charlotte Convention Center; and two in the six blocks between Seventh, East Trade, South Caldwell, and the planned trolley line. Razing the Hive in the suburbs and rebuilding on that site was the sixth consideration. Each site had 10 to 12 acres of land and multiple owners, except the Hive site that was already owned by the city (see Exhibit 7.22). Individuals owned 0.25 to 1.5 acre parcels in the uptown locations. The locations were selected by the subcommittee based on the criteria; no one was going to "make a killing" in a land sale deal.

Deliberations of the New Arena Subcommittee on Finance

Independence Arena originally cost $5.5 million to build in 1951. From 1992 to 1993, an additional $6.6 million was spent on renovations and repairs to enable the Charlotte Checkers hockey team and the UNC Charlotte 49ers (basketball) to play there. Its assessed value in 1998 was $14.6 million.

The Hive was built in 1988 with $47.4 million in bonds, $56.9 million in construction costs, $9.34 million in changes to adapt to professional basketball, $116,500 in land value, $28.1 million in interest payments, and $10 million in improvements for a total investment of $94.9 million. In 1998, the assessed value of the Hive was $62.4 million. The amount still owed on the bonds in 1998 was $32.5 million.

Exhibit 7.21   Recommended Arena Sites

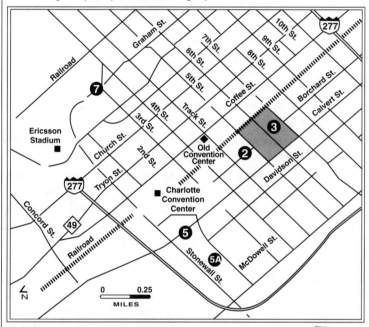

Recommended Arena Sites

Here are the possible sites for a new Hornets arena that will be forwarded to the Charlotte City Council on June 28. The sites include the Charlotte Coliseum land, where the team now plays. The New Arena Committee may add or subtract sites from this list, but for the past few weeks the group's location subcommittee has focused on the following five uptown parcels, which are grouped into three areas:

Site 2 and 3
• Pros: Centrally located. Plenty of parking. Trolley will run next to it.
• Cons: Major streets may have to be closed or rerouted. Property
            now held by many different owners.

Site 5 and 5a
• Pros: Could complement Convention Center. Easy highway access.
• Cons: Convention Center expansion planned for Site 5.

Site 7
• Pros: Could play off Ericsson Stadium next door, creating an uptown
            "sports neighborhood." Plenty of room. Good highway access.
            May also be able to build baseball stadium nearby.
• Cons: Some streets may need to be closed or rerouted.

New Arena Projected Costs. The proposed new arena was expected to cost approximately $171.5 million to construct plus another $30 million for interest on loans or bonds. The location could add considerably to the cost. Uptown locations would be more expensive than where the

Exhibit 7.22   Arena Site Characteristics

Site	Number Parcels Owned	Total Acreage
New arena site # 2	26	12.296
New arena site # 3	46	12.616
New arena site # 5	4	10.260
New arena site # 7	19	11.844
Current Coliseum site	1	12.100

Source: City of Charlotte documents.

Hive was located because the city owned the land on which the Hive was situated; all uptown sites would include acquisition of several parcels from multiple landowners.

In addition, unanticipated factors began to influence the deliberations and recommendations regarding financing a new arena. The 1998–1999 season was not great for any of the NBA teams because of the lock-out shortened season; however, the Hornets seemed to have suffered more than most other teams. The Hornets had a 27% drop in per game turnstile attendance during the season, whereas the league's average drop was 2.2%. The Hornets drew 316,169 fans over 25 games during the 1998–1999 season (not including playoff games) compared to an average of 17,327 fans per game during 1997–1998. On average there were 4,700 fewer fans per game in the 1998–1999 season compared to 1997–1998. Road trips were no better according to a *Street & Smith's Sports Business Journal* report that Charlotte was the third-worst road draw in the league.

Ticket Sales Begin to Decline. According to the NBA, Charlotte led the league in ticket sales for the first eight of its ten years as a franchise. The NBA tracks ticket sales, not turnstile attendance figures. However, after the 1998–1999 season, the team ranked sixth in ticket sales with an average of 19,232 tickets sold per game (actual turnstile attendance per game was lower as many fans chose not to attend the game). The number of no-shows directly affected the Authority's revenues. According to the Authority's managing director, "It's clear we're going to lose some ground because of the late start [because of the player strike] and the softer attendance."

In May 1999, the New Arena Committee's financial subcommittee voted 4 to 3 to recommend that the Hornets pay 70% of the costs of a new arena and the city pay the other 30%. Earlier in the meeting the financial subcommittee voted 4 to 3 to reject a 60/40% split between the Hornets and the city. For a $200 to $250 million arena, the Hornets would pay between $140 and $175 million under the 70/30 proposal.

The Hornets Organization Responds to the Finance Committee Proposal. The Hornets organization was quick to reject the 70/30 proposal. "To be honest with you, 60/40 doesn't work either," said Hornets' vice president for finance, Wayne DeBlander. He argued that the Hornets simply could not afford the plan. "It needs to be something where it provides the sports franchise with some ability to pay its bills, its debts, and to have something left over to make it all worth it."

Hornets management explained that the Hornets' operating expenses had been increasing at a rate that was faster than the rate of revenue growth. They provided data to the New Arena Committee in a percentage format because the team was wholly owned by Shinn and its income was merged into his personal income (see Exhibits 7.23 and 7.24 for illustrations of the Hornets' financial dilemma).

DeBlander suggested that the Hornets contribute amounts between $60 and $80 million. Recent arenas constructed in Miami and Indianapolis that also had only one tenant included slightly over 50% of the total costs being contributed by the team involved.

The NBA team's organization further argued that the WNBA Sting (women's professional basketball), the Checkers (currently playing at Independence Arena), indoor soccer, arena football, ACC events, NCAA events, and other venues such as concerts, ice capades, and the circus would use the facility. "With such widespread community use, the new arena should be financed by both the Hornets and the City," DeBlander concluded.

❖ THE NEW ARENA COMMITTEE REPORT

The committee reported on June 28, 1999, that it had unanimous agreement for its recommendations that were outcomes of the three

Exhibit 7.23   Charlotte Hornets Net Income and Cash Flow as Compared to
Break Even for Fiscal Years 1988–1989 Through 1997–1998

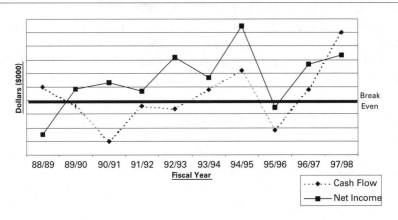

Note A: The Charlotte Hornets franchise is a partnership. Accordingly,
income tax expense is not recorded in the financial statements of
the Hornets. Rather, the operating results of the Hornets are
included in the income tax returns of the partners. As George
Shinn owns 100% of the Hornets, the results are included in his
personal income tax returns. The amounts needed to pay taxes are
distributed to him, as needed, and are part of the aggregate cash
flow adjustment shown above.

Note B: Cash flow adjustments include, among other things, approximately
$2.2 million annually for the reduction of long-term debt for the
Hornets.

Note C: Approximately $7.5 million of the cash flow adjustments during
fiscal 1990/1991 were to redeem partnership interests.

Note D: Net income and cash flows for fiscal year 1994/1995 were
positively impacted by the receipt of expansion revenue.

Note E: Cash flow for fiscal year 1997/1998 was positively affected by
proceeds from the sale of the Charlotte Knights.

Source: Charlotte Hornets document supplied to the New Arena
Committee.

subcommittees' research and study. It would now be up to the council
to decide on the next steps and ultimately whether the city should be
involved in building a new arena.

   The Size and Design Subcommittee worked under three basic
assumptions:

Exhibit 7.24   Hornets Total Revenue Compared to League-Wide Average
per Team Total Revenue

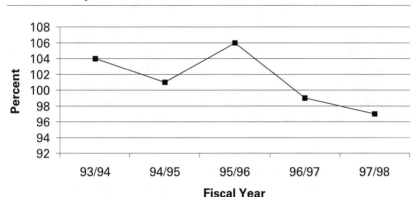

Annually, the NBA creates a statement of average league-wide financial
information and compares the league-wide average to each franchise's
actual results. Generally, the Hornets' actual revenues have been above the
league-wide average. The chart above shows how the Hornets compare to
that average over the past five fiscal years. The 100% line represents the
league-wide average.

Source: Charlotte Hornets document supplied to the New Arena
Committee.

1. Any new arena should be built with the primary focus of hosting the tenants and events that were currently accommodated in
Charlotte. In addition, the arena should be able to accommodate other
events that might be attracted to Charlotte in the future.

2. Although the primary focus should be on Charlotte's professional basketball teams (i.e., the Charlotte Hornets and WNBA
Charlotte Sting) as the primary tenants, it was clear that this arena
must be able to accommodate other events held in Charlotte. These
events included the ACC tournament, NCAA tournaments, concerts,
family shows, and circuses.

3. The arena should be developed with enough flexibility to
accommodate potential future uses, such as professional hockey (NHL
or minor league team). Other professional, amateur, or spectator events
to consider included indoor soccer, arena football, tennis, volleyball,
and various corporate or religious meetings.

The subcommittee recommended and the committee agreed that a new arena should have a minimum site of approximately five acres, containing about 750,000 square feet of space with a facility footprint (actual building dimensions) of approximately 500 feet by 500 feet. The arena should encompass enough space to allow for future expansion of various arena components, if they were financially viable. Ample parking should be in close proximity, and the arena should be sited to promote synergies with properties within the area including the New Charlotte Convention Center, hotels, restaurants, and Ericsson Stadium. The development should provide an area of green or open space that could be used to help alleviate pedestrian congestion and would provide a park environment in the uptown area.

The committee recommended a seating capacity of approximately 20,000 seats to provide an appropriate blend of seating and intimacy for NBA basketball and most other events. However, given the importance of the ACC men's basketball tournament and the rich history Charlotte had in hosting the ACC and NCAA tournament events, the arena design should be flexible enough to accommodate the seating requirements of these tournaments and the other Coliseum events that required in excess of 20,000 seats. In addition, given their importance to the revenue-generating ability of the building, the arena should incorporate up to 80 private suites (with the ability to expand the inventory if demand warranted) and approximately 2,500 club seats, depending on the market demand.

Further, the committee recommended that an initial construction cost budget should be established consistent with other new state-of-the-art arenas. Certain project-related costs including land acquisition, infrastructure, and parking should be provided in a manner that minimizes the amount of city funds necessary to develop the project.

Facility components included: (a) those that were essential to the program needs of the arena and its tenant; and (b) those that were considered nonessential items or enhancements. These nonessential elements should be considered and assigned priority as costs allowed or be added through other private investment sources.

Essential Components
   Team locker rooms
   Team training area (with adequate medical, training and x-ray equipment)
   Public first aid stations

On-site storage
On-site media facilities
Truck docks and trash service
Restrooms
Media facilities
Box office
Sponsorship areas
Administrative offices for the Hornets Authority, concession
operations and arena operations

Enhancements
Team practice court
Public restaurants
Meeting rooms/banquet rooms
Business center
Interactive areas
Production studios
Membership clubs
Health club
Museum/hall of fame
Other nonteam retail that could enhance the viability of the
arena and area

The committee concluded that a new building should incorporate
the appropriate level of other building components (special lighting,
power distribution, air handling, audio, visual, security, telecommunications, and computer equipment) consistent with other new arenas.
As it relates to essential facility components, the new arena should be
designed to incorporate industry standards and ratios with regard to
the applicable facility components. Such standards and ratios should
be integral components of the facility's design. The subcommittee
believed that it was important to design the arena so that it allowed
enough space for future expansion of various facility components, if
deemed financially viable.

The Site Subcommittee had studied arena locations in other cities.
The majority of arenas (16 of 25 or 68%) were located in downtown
areas (see Exhibit 7.11). Of the arenas constructed after 1990, 80% were
in downtown areas. The subcommittee used the following factors to
determine rankings for the sites identified: street/road capacity

(ingress and egress), timing/availability, traffic impact on adjacent areas, ownership complexity, transit availability, size and configuration, parking availability and location, relocation of existing businesses, pedestrian access, constructability, safety (perception of area), environmental considerations, zoning, compatibility of use to surrounding area, availability of utilities, adjacent land use, relocation/abandonment of roads, availability and synergy of support services, roadway redevelopment, visibility/image, sidewalks, on-site development opportunities, surrounding area development opportunities, proximity and synergism to other facilities, national compatibility with neighborhood and areas, regional compatibility with corporate environment, local compatibility with other planning issues, marketability of facility/events, facility economics, acquisition, impact on economics of the area and city tax revenues, infrastructure, NBA team/other tenants, and potential cost offsets.

The subcommittee decided to provide the city council with a listing of sites that could potentially accommodate a new multipurpose arena, rather than provide a specific ranking of the individual sites. This would allow the city council flexibility in choosing a site for the arena, and provide for further evaluation of a variety of issues including land availability, infrastructure requirements, land and infrastructure cost, other city planning initiatives and other similar issues. To develop this listing, the individual scores were evaluated for each of the eight categories based on the specific rankings of each subcategory. The average ranking was calculated for each site as well as a list of advantages and disadvantages for each of the five endorsed sites. The subcommittee understood that the cost of each parcel would be a factor in the decision and wanted the city council to have as much information as possible about each of the sites, in case a reasonable price could not be negotiated for a particular one.

The Finance Subcommittee's recommendations were endorsed by the committee. The subcommittee agreed about several general ideas: The city should strive to maximize private-sector participation in the new arena project while recognizing that some level of public participation would be required. The subcommittee believed that the mix of public and private investment in the new arena should be in line with similar recent NBA arena projects in other cities. Finally, the subcommittee believed that as a result of the long-term commitment of the

NBA to the Charlotte region, other public beneficiaries of the project, including Mecklenburg County and the state, should participate in the public/private partnership to build a new arena.

As the primary user of the potential arena, the subcommittee believed the Hornets would be the primary beneficiary of a new arena and should provide a significant contribution that would be consistent with other NBA franchise/arena investments. Other new arenas were financed by the franchise in a range from a low of 0% in Minnesota to a high of 100% in Boston for the Fleet Center and in Toronto for the Air Canada Centre. Overall, the percentage of franchise/arena participation approximated 74%, 58.5% for single tenant arenas and 83% for dual-purpose arenas. The public traditionally funded most of the remaining percentage of the project costs. As such, for a single tenant arena, the public funded approximately 41.5%.

Recent arena costs were studied. They ranged from a low of $84.7 million for the Target Center (1990) in Minneapolis to a high of $376.0 million for the Staples Center in Los Angeles (1999). The cost for NBA-only arenas averaged approximately $155 million, whereas the average increased to $238 million for NBA/NHL arenas. The subcommittee noted that it was difficult to draw accurate comparisons among individual arena developments because of the different completion dates as well as labor, materials, and other similar costs that were specific to each market.

Given the aforementioned considerations coupled with the operating recommendations and assuming a total project cost of between $200 and $250 million, the subcommittee believed that a public-sector investment (including all project beneficiaries such as city, county, and state) of $80 to $100 million was a useful estimate. It was consistent with other comparable public-sector investments in NBA arenas and was comparable to the public participation in Ericsson Stadium (Charlotte's football stadium), adjusted for inflation. Based on funding sources used by other NBA teams, the Hornets' participation could be from: premium seating, naming rights, other arena and team revenue sources (equity), lease payments, revenue sharing, or personal seat licenses.

In addition, the subcommittee felt that other private-sector beneficiaries of the project should be called on to fund a portion of the arena project costs similar to downtown arena projects in Cleveland and Indianapolis. Private-sector participation would serve to solidify the commitment to a new arena and the economic benefits that over 100 annual usage days and 1.0 million people would have on the surrounding area. Such investments might be in the form of land donation, parking, off-site improvements, direct investment, or other methods. The subcommittee believed that it was incumbent on the city to take a leadership role in involving the county, state, and to the extent possible, federal participation in the uptown arena project. Although not likely, federal urban development funds had been used in some cities to defray some costs associated with arena projects.

The sources that the subcommittee felt the city could pursue for funding a portion of the arena project included proceeds from the sale of the Hive and old convention center sites, ticket surcharge, rental car tax, or certain specific existing municipal debt service funds. The subcommittee strongly believed that general property taxes, even those associated with the municipal debt service fund, should not be used as a potential revenue source for a new arena. The subcommittee preferred that users of the new arena bear most of the costs that the public would bear, rather than the general population through their property tax levies. If the debt service fund were used, other revenue sources that were allocated to the fund such as sales tax, occupancy tax, or other nonproperty tax revenues should be specifically earmarked for debt reduction associated with the new arena. Construction risks and cost overruns could have a significant impact on the ultimate costs of a new facility such as the proposed new arena; therefore, the subcommittee believed that such risk should be the responsibility of the third-party construction firm or the team, not the city.

For purposes of developing a financial model, it was assumed that the arena would be publicly owned and the new arena would not be subject to property (ad valorem) taxes. The subcommittee discussed the advantages and disadvantages of management of the arena by the Hornets, the Authority, or shared operations between the two entities but did not make a recommendation as the issue would probably have an impact on the level of private funding associated with the new arena. Further, Independence Arena might affect the operations of the new uptown arena. It was the concern of the subcommittee that a number of events, which would use Independence Arena, potentially might not use a new arena because of the cost, scheduling conflicts, and size if Independence Arena were closed.

❖ THE VOTE

Under the 1998 Agreement between the city and the Hornets, the city council had until December 2000 to determine if the city would participate in building a new arena. The December 1998 deadline and the July 1999 deadline were met. The December 1999 city council meeting was nearing conclusion. Important decisions had to be made that would set in motion various activities to initiate construction in December 2000. The councilmembers were to decide on whether to proceed with a partnership, and if so on a specific site for the new arena, its size and design, and the most controversial—the method of financing.

A majority of the council was already on record stating that if they voted for any public funding, then a plan had to be designed to involve public participation in some manner. The council could vote tonight to build a new arena. Alternatively, they could vote to place the issue on a public referendum ballot for citizens to decide. If the decision to participate in funding a new arena were negative, Shinn had clearly stated that he would move the Hornets away from Charlotte to another venue. From a political standpoint, it would be safer for the councilmembers to allow the general public to vote on the decision to involve the city in a new arena project. On the other hand, a referendum would take significantly longer to reach a decision and the delay itself could result in the city losing the Hornets along with the revenues and prestige that accompanied the team's presence in Charlotte.

Mayor McCrory looked around the packed meeting room and rapped his gavel. "Are we ready to vote?"

❖ NOTES

Chapter Source: *Case Research Journal,* Published by the North American Case Research Association, a Pearson Custom Publication, David W. Rosenthal, Editor.

1. Estimate provided by UNC Charlotte professor John Connaughton, PhD, in a study commissioned by the Charlotte Hornets in 1998.

❖   REFERENCES

Baade, R. A. (1994). *Stadiums, professional sports, and economic development: Assessing the reality.* Detroit, MI: Heartland Institute.

Gould Media Services. (1997). *Revenues from sports venues.* York, ME: Gould Media Services.

Marvin, T. E. (1995). *The site location process of the Charlotte coliseum: Did it serve the public interest?* Unpublished thesis, Master's of Public Administration, University of North Carolina at Charlotte.

Rafool, M. (1997). *Playing the stadium game: Financing professional sports facilities in the 90's.* National Conference of State Legislatures, Legislative Finance Papers (March), No. 106.

Who pulls 'em in on the road. (1998). *Street & Smith's Sports Business Journal, 1*(42), 17.

8

Smart Cards for Paperless Transactions

Facilitation of e-Government
or Threat to Security?

Cheryl L. Brown

❖ **BACKGROUND**

Parliamentary debate in Malaysia has heightened attention about the future of Malaysia's Government Multi-Purpose Card (GMPC), touted as the world's first public-sector, multi-application smart card. A member of the Malaysian parliament, Chang See Ten, expressed his concern about potential abuse of card information by syndicates. "Since the card is also a passport and an identity card, there may be threats to the country's security if the card is abused."

Energy, Communications and Multimedia Ministry parliamentary secretary Chia Kwang Chye replied, "The cards have security features." Moreover, he added, "The government will also introduce the Personal Data Protection Act."

Since the card's introduction to the Malaysian public on April 12, 2001, the National Registration Department (NRD) has maintained that the GMPC did not pose a security threat. "The public should not be unduly worried about security risks affecting the country's new 'smart' identity card, . . . as it is very safe," declared Nur Ashikin Othman, NRD public relations officer (Streejit, 2001).

Data in the smart card was either "open" or "protected," she added. "Open" data was general personal data, such as name, address, identity card number, and driver's license information. "Protected" information was sensitive data, such as medical records.

Nur Ashikin reported that to ensure data security of the GMPC, the card used an authentication system of cryptography for secure key management, an operating system with firewalls to separate each application, and writer-disablement of nonchangeable, critical data such as name and date of birth after data entry to avoid changes.

The GMPC offered an access key to transactions of e-government to achieve Malaysia's goal of a paperless government and facilitate e-services to citizens via six applications. It would replace the Malaysian identity card and driver's license paper documents. Additional government applications of the GMPC were passport information and health data. One of the nongovernment applications of the GMPC was e-cash to facilitate efficiency and delivery of public and payment services; Public Key Infrastructure (PKI), which would allow users to conduct secured e-commerce and transactions using digital certificate via networks such as the Internet, was another application tentatively scheduled for addition. The security risks of the multipurpose card and other factors, however, may thwart its universal proliferation.

❖ OVERVIEW OF MALAYSIA

Located in Southeast Asia, Malaysia consists of two regions separated by approximately 640 miles of the South China Sea. The two land masses consist of the peninsula bordering Thailand and the northern one-third of the island of Borneo, bordering Brunei, Indonesia, and the South China Sea. The total area of land and water is 329,750 square kilometers, slightly larger than New Mexico. The Federation of Malaysia was established in 1963 through the merging of Malaya (independent from British rule in 1957 when it became what is now Peninsular Malaysia) and the former British Singapore, both of which formed Western Malaysia, and the Sabah and Sarawak in north Borneo, which composed East Malaysia. Singapore separated from the federation in 1965. The conventional shortened name of the country is Malaysia.

More than half of Malaysia's population of 22,229,040 (July 2001 estimate) is Malay. Along with the oldest indigenous people, they represented 58% of the population and formed the *bumiputera*, which translated as "sons" or "princes of the soil." Among the remaining population, 27% is Chinese, 8% Indian, and 7% other nationalities. The Chinese are Malaysia's wealthiest community, but the Malays dominate politically. The main religion is Islam, which is practiced by more than half of the population. Other religions include Buddhism, Daoism, Hinduism, Christianity, Sikhism, and Shamanism, which is practiced in East Malaysia.

The country's official language is Bahasa Melayu, but English, Chinese dialects (Cantonese, Mandarin, Hokkien, Hakka, Hainan, Foochow), Tamil, Telugu, Malayalam, Panjabi, and Thai are spoken. In addition, several indigenous languages, mainly Iban and Kadazan, are spoken in East Malaysia.

Malaysia is a federation of states governed by a constitutional monarchy with a bicameral parliament or Parlimen consisting of a non-elected senate or Dewan Negara (69 seats—43 appointed by the paramount ruler and 26 appointed by the state legislatures) and a house of representatives or Dewan Rakyat (193 seats—members are elected by popular vote, which favored the rural Malay population, to serve five years). The head of state is the Supreme Head of the Federation and is selected by and from nine hereditary sultans, or rulers. The Raja of Perlis, Tuanku Syed Sirajuddin, was chosen by secret ballot to be Malaysia's twelfth monarch, taking over after the death of Salahuddin Abdul Aziz Shah in November 2001.

The prime minister exercises executive power. In 2001, Dr. Mahathir bin Mohamad was the head of government and leader of the majority party (United Malays National Organization) or coalition in the house of representatives. He was appointed by the head of state. He governed with the assistance of an appointed ministerial cabinet. Prime Minister Mahathir was Southeast Asia's longest-serving leader. He had been Malaysia's prime minister since 1981, but not without controversy. He had criticized large, industrialized countries for dominating economic trade groupings and excluding the voice of small, less-developed countries. Mahathir had also openly criticized Western powers for failing to control currency leaders who he blamed for Asia's financial crisis in the late 1990s. He had received criticism for intolerance against opponents and control of the media. The highlight of his leadership had been the push to fully develop Malaysia by 2020 and to make it an information technology leader in the global arena.

Malaysia's administrative divisions, along with population listings, are the Federal Territory of Kuala Lumpur (1,297,526), Federal Territory of Labuan (70,517), and 13 states: Johor (2,565,701), Kedah (1,572,107), Kelantan (1,289,199), Melaka (602,867), Negeri Sembilan (830,080), Pahang (1,231,176), Perak (2,030,382), Perlis (198,335), Pinang (1,225,501), Selangor (3,947,527), and Terengganu (879,691) in West Malaysia, and Sabah (2,449,389) and Sarawak (2,012,616) in East Malaysia. The capital of Malaysia is Kuala Lumpur, commonly referred to as "KL," but the administrative seat of government is Putrajaya, the new Administrative Centre of the Federal Government of Malaysia. It is situated within the Multimedia Super Corridor (MSC), the information technology complex of Malaysia.

❖ WHAT IS A SMART CARD?

An integrated circuit card (ICC), more commonly referred to as a smart card, is a plastic device about the size of a standard credit card that contains an embedded microprocessor and a memory chip, or only a memory chip with nonprogrammable logic. The chip, or engine room of the card, is the *smart* part of the device. The microprocessor card can add, delete, and process data on the card. This type of smart card can store more data than a magnetic stripe card, and it can be programmed for different applications (generally referred to as the programs or software that the integrated circuit of the card implemented) or reprogrammed to add, delete, or rearrange data. Memory-only chip cards have storage space for data, but they have no processor on the card to manipulate the data. It is, therefore, dependent on the card acceptance device (CAD) or card reader for its processing. This kind of smart card, such as a prepaid phone card, can only implement a predefined operation. Smart card vendors expected microprocessor smart cards to supplant memory chip cards by 2005.

Some cards contain programming and data to support multiple applications, and others can be updated to add new applications after they are issued. Although the memory capacity is currently up to 32K of data space, Samsung Electronics Co. Ltd. in 2000 was developing a next-generation smart card chip with a higher memory capacity

(Global Sources Security & Safety, 2000). SchlumbergerSema claimed it had a 64K card and a 128K model (Caterinicchia, 2001). Smart cards were contact or contactless cards. Contact cards can be designed to be inserted into a slot and read by a special smart card reader. Contactless smart cards are designed to be read at a distance, such as at a toll booth. Cards can be disposable or reloadable (for most applications). Some cards have a time period for renewal to ensure the card stays intact.

A major challenge of smart cards has been the lack of interoperability. Different cards have usually not been interchangeable. Many smart card analysts and researchers argued that lack of standards for smart cards has impeded their widespread use. Although the International Standards Organization (ISO) provides standards, variations among cards exist in their physical dimensions, location of contacts, and agreement in the security domain.

Authenticating the cardholder's identity, another concern, has relied primarily on using the cardholder's personal identification number (PIN), which the cardholder must remember and type in upon request. The main disadvantage of the PIN is its risk of being abused, stolen, or forgotten. Measurement of a single or combined form of physiological or behavioral characteristics unique to the cardholder has emerged as a more secure form of cardholder verification. This method used biometrics of fingerprints, thumbprints, hand prints, palm or face geometry, voice patterns, iris and retinal scans, signature verification, and keystroke dynamics. Many countries and institutions use biometric systems to authenticate cardholder identity; however, in some political cultures, citizens view the use of biometrics for smart cards as an invasion of privacy or excessive control over information on the part of the government. In the wake of the September 11, 2001, terrorist attacks in the United States, the public and private sectors readdressed the topic of smart cards for immigration data and airport security.

Multipurpose Card

A smart card is advantageous and cost-effective when capable of storing data related to more than one function and more than one application. By 2001, the use of multipurpose cards was increasing in countries as national identification cards emerged capable of additional applications such as e-cash transactions, e-government services, e-medical records, or passport documents. Most smart card consultants and researchers recommended multipurpose cards for cost-efficiency, convenience, and likely acceptance by the public. In commenting on post-September 11 discussions in the United States and the United Kingdom about national identification cards for tightening security, Jan Van Arkel, cochair of the eEurope Smart Card Charter, which was part of the European Commission's e-commerce initiative, stated: "It would be difficult to justify the cost of a chip card for just security purposes. It would also have too much resistance from citizens. Offering a card that provides greater security plus additional services, such as e-government, would have a chance of being approved" (Bowen, 2001). A report released by the Progressive Policy Institute, affiliated with the Democratic Leadership Council of the United States, recommended that any smart card or biometric solutions sponsored by government funding offer multiple applications with compatibility and interoperability with other government and commercial areas and not just airports and airlines (Atkinson, 2001).

In a press briefing on April 12, 2001, Malaysia introduced the first public-sector, multi-application card, promising an access key to transactions of e-government to achieve Malaysia's goal of a paperless government and facilitating e-services to the citizens via six applications. Before April, a single card served as the Malaysian identity card and driver's license, replacing two former documents: the plastic-based National Identification Card and the paper-based, laminated driver's license. Additional government applications of the GMPC will be passport information and health data. The health data will be write-protected once it is entered, and when the application is fully operational. The two nongovernment applications of the GMPC are e-cash to facilitate efficiency and delivery of public and payment services, and PKI to allow users to conduct secured e-commerce and transactions using digital certificate via networks such as the Internet.

As of December 2001, these applications were not fully operational. Although the initial use of the card was in a restricted area of Malaysia, the affluent Klang Valley, national roll-out was targeted for 2003 with anticipated completion in five to eight years. Parliamentary debate raised the issue of security risks of the cards. Those risks, along with a bevy of concerns—privacy, scalability, accessibility, information technology, cost, and politics—might thwart universal proliferation of the card.

Prime Minister Mahathir assigned a special committee, MyKad Evaluation Taskforce (MET), to evaluate the GMPC in its current use and to prepare a set of recommendations to present to the national government on the implementation of the universal roll-out of the GMPC. The MET was composed of the prime minister; governor of the Central Bank of Malaysia; the secretary general of the Ministry of Home Affairs; the director general of the NRD; representatives from the NRD, Road Transportation Department (RTD), Royal Malaysian Police (RMP), Ministry of Health (MOH), and Immigration Department (IMM); and three voluntary members of the MSC International Advisory Panel (see www.mdc.com.my for IAP list).

❖ MYKAD

The official name of Malaysia's GMPC became "MyKad" at its international launch at the Putra World Trade Centre on September 5, 2001, which coincided with the fifth annual meeting of the MSC International Advisory Panel. "My" refers to Malaysia's Internet country code and to personal ownership. "Kad" is an acronym for two terms: "Kad Akuan Diri," which translates as "personal identification card," and "Kad Aplikasi Digital," which translates as "digital application card" and also means card. The official Web site for MyKad (jpn.gov.my/gmpc/GMPC.htm) debuted on August 29, 2001, to allow the public to access information about the features, benefits, reader devices, application process, replacement process, calendar of events, and benefits of the GMPC.

Any citizen or permanent resident of Malaysia aged 12 years or older was eligible to apply for MyKad at any Government Service Centre (GSC), a one-stop location for any service related to MyKad. Applicants had to have supporting documents—national identification card, driver's license (if in ownership), child's birth certificate, and national identification card of either parent or sponsor for a nonadult applicant, and a machine-readable passport (if in ownership) to upload passport data to MyKad. Data collected at the GSC was transmitted to the NRD for verification before it was submitted for personalization and card production. In the personalization stage, data file contents and application data were written to the card. Also, cardholder identity information was stored. Then a utilization lock was written to indicate the card was in the utilization phase. Following data verification and personalization, the card was sent to the specified GSC for the applicant. The GSCs were also available to cardholders to renew a lost card, renew the driver's license, update card information, upload passport information, and pay and update summonses.

Carrying a card was not new to Malaysian citizens and residents. MyKad's anchor source was the paper-based identification cards introduced in 1946, when Malaysia first started registering all citizens over 12 years of age. One of the links to the MyKad official site showed the evolution of the identification card over the years of 1948, 1960, 1990, 1999, and 2001. The government was aware, however, that people might not fully accept the use of a *single card* for *many purposes*. During the gradual roll-out of the card in 2001 and 2002, the NRD used television and radio advertisements and nationwide road shows (crucial for reaching villages), along with the official Web site, to encourage use of MyKad. The card was not mandatory at the time of its introduction, but the government amended the National Registration Act to officially recognize MyKad as the national identity card of Malaysia in June 2001. After this date, anyone who needed to reapply for a national identification card because of loss or damage, or who applied for an identity card for the first time, was required to get the GMPC. For many people receiving the card in 2001, only the identification card application was available. This single application card looked exactly like the multi-application card. Other applications would be added as the national roll-out developed and the related infrastructure was ready.

MyKad Applications

MyKad was designed to offer six applications on a single technology platform. The first application of MyKad was the identification card, which used microprocessor chip and biometrics technology. The identification card number was a PIN number for a secure access key to other applications and systems as added. The second application was a driver's license, which replaced the previous license and functioned as a regular driver's license. It provided full driving records for enforcement officers and traffic police reviewing the data (*only* the driving-related data) as necessary. The third application was passport data. It was a supplement to, *not replacement* for, the Malaysian international passport. Malaysian citizens still had to carry a passport when entering and exiting the country in overseas travel. This application, however, facilitated entry and exit at immigration checkpoints, and the biometrics technology enhanced airport security. Also, having the immigration number on the card offered additional information that could be useful for other government agencies.

MyKad's fourth application was health data. The smart card chip stored basic and vital medical information, which could improve health care in emergency and general medical situations and improve overall diagnosis. The data could also facilitate health care visits without completing a mound of paperwork. Once the information was entered, it was write-protected and could not be changed. Firewalls offered privacy and security by separating the applications. Traffic officers would not be able to access health data. A fifth application of the evolving smart card was e-cash, which enabled cardholders to make small purchases when the card was accepted. The Malaysian Electronic Payment System (MEPS), formed by a consortium of 24 Malaysian financial institutions and the operators of automated teller machines (ATMs), offered a cash application that allowed cardholders to load RM500 (Malaysia's currency) into their cards and spend it at participating stores. The sixth application was the PKI, which allowed users to conduct secure transactions and e-commerce using a digital certificate over the Internet and similar networks.

Malaysia planned to offer additional applications to MyKad. As Deputy Prime Minister Abdullah Ahmad Badawi stated, "Life will be easier with the GMPC . . . one day you can even swipe the card to enter your room. We will add more applications when all the systems are in place" (Matthews, 2001).

Reading the data on MyKad required a CAD. It enabled the officials of authorized government departments to access specific information in the card related to a particular department. The type of CAD varied according to the user and need. Cardholders could also access data. A personal Key Ring Reader (KRR) gave citizens access to general data stored in the chip, or cardholders could check the data on their card at public Chip Data Verifier (CDV) kiosks. A desktop PC-version CDV allowed all data in the card's memory to be displayed to check for accuracy. A more powerful KRR was available for an enforcement office to access specific data in the card. A Mobile CAD was not only able to read cardholder information but was also able to conduct 1:1 fingerprint verification and give authentication. Enforcement officers from different government agencies used the Mobile CAD to carry out related activities. A Secure Access Module was available in the Mobile CAD to offer secure information access.

The Autogate was used to facilitate exit and reentry of cardholder Malaysians at Malaysian immigration checkpoints. It required 10 seconds or less to pick up the data in the card; the manual process required 45 seconds. The NRD and card supporters maintained that the technology of MyKad increased the efficiency of immigration processing without risking national security.

Broader Scope of the Card

Malaysia's cutting-edge technology of the GMPC fit the broader plan of the nation to become a fully developed country by 2020. Prime Minister Mahathir introduced Vision 2020 in 1991, as a plan to bring Malaysia into advanced technological development. In speaking before the Malaysian Business Council about Vision 2020, Mahathir asserted, "In a world of high technology Malaysia cannot afford to lag behind. We cannot be in the front line of modern technology but we must always try to catch up in those fields where we may have certain advantages" (Mahathir, 1991).

MyKad signaled a crucial turning point in another development-related initiative—the MSC—launched in 1996. Prime Minister Mahathir introduced and labeled the corridor as "the global facilitator of the Information Age" (Mahathir, 1995). The MSC, located on 750 square kilometers of land in a corridor south of Kuala Lumpur, was designed with state-of-the-art technology to attract software firms, telecommunications experts, and multimedia companies. An international advisory panel, with a membership that had included Bill Gates of Microsoft, Lou Gertsner of IBM, and other top-echelon IT experts, had offered global input on strategic issues. The MSC had two intelligent cities. One of these cities, Cyberjaya, consisted of multimedia industries, R&D centers, Multimedia University, and operations headquarters for multinational companies. Putrajaya, the other intelligent city, was the new administrative center of government and the start-up of electronic government for Malaysia. As a means to facilitate e-government and other e-services, the MSC had implemented the GMPC as the first of its seven flagship applications. The GMPC was designed as a tool and medium for citizens to interface with other government applications of the six forthcoming MSC flagship initiatives: e-government, smart schools, telehealth, borderless marketing centers, worldwide manufacturing webs, and R&D clusters.

Collaborative Effort for Mykad

As one of the MSC flagship applications, the overall implementation of MyKad was under a tightly organized structure to ensure the

GMPC project was implemented as a national vision and plan. (See organizational chart at: www.jpn.gov.my/gmpc/GMPC.htm.) The top tier of the structure was the MSC Implementation Council Meeting chaired by Prime Minister Mahathir. The second level was the Multipurpose Card Steering Committee chaired by the governor of Bank Negara (the Central Bank of Malaysia), Dr. Zeti Akhtar Aziz. She became the bank governor in May 2000. The Central Bank was the financial advisor and bank for the government. The third level were two committees overseeing the implementation of Malaysia's two cards—the GMPC and the Payment Multipurpose Card (PMC) with applications integrated into the GMPC. The committees were the PMC Taskforce and GMPC Taskforce. The GMPC Taskforce, chaired by Secretary General of Home Affairs Datuk Aseh Che Mat, handled coordination of the government agencies involved in implementation of MyKad. On the fourth level was the GMPC Project Management Committee, chaired by NRD Director General Datuk Azizan Ayob. The GMPC Implementation Team, chaired by GMPC Project Director Wan Mohamed Ariffin bin Wan Ismail of the NRD, and the GMPC Unit were at the fifth level of the implementation structure, representing the basic level of implementing the project. As director of the GMPC project, Wan Mohamed Ariffin had been a point-of-contact for international press interviews and smart card conferences to present information on the GMPC.

Government agencies involved in the planning, development, and implementation of the GMPC project included the NRD, as the lead agency of the project, RTD, RMP, MOH, and IMM. The GMPC project also received cooperation from 14 additional agencies in Malaysia, including the Bank Negara Malaysia and the Multimedia Development Corporation (the overseer of the MSC).

In addition to the public sector, private-sector participants collaborated in the development of MyKad as members of the GMPC Consortium. In May 1999, the government of Malaysia awarded the development project to the GMPC Consortium after a thorough evaluation of submitted proposals. The consortium consisted of five companies that supplied technology for MyKad. CSA (MSC) Sdn Bhd had the responsibility to design, install, and commission IT infrastructure related to local area network (LAN) and wide area network (WAN). Dibena Enterprise Sdn Bhd was the system hardware provider for the central insurance system personalization equipment. EPNCR Sdn Bhd had the responsibility of supplying, installing, and integrating CADs and biometric devices. Iris Technologies Sdh Bhn contributed as the card manufacturer and developer and provider of smart card solutions for the GMPC project. It also provided card personalization services. Iris Technologies worked with MEPS to implement the Proton e-purse (MEPS cash or e-cash). Unisys offered project management and system integration for the GMPC project.

❖ WHAT DID THE MULTIPURPOSE
    CARD OFFER MALAYSIA?

MyKad offered Malaysia several advantages in terms of practicality, cost-effectiveness, efficiency, paperless government, security, and leadership.

Practicality

From the practical perspective, MyKad offered the convenience of carrying one card. Although all applications had not been uploaded and the card was not universal, it had the potential to offer an all-in-one smart card, with adaptability and interoperability for additional applications and functions. Already it eliminated the need for both a national identification card and a driver's license. The chip stored all of the identity data including birth date, birthplace, information, two thumbprint minutiae, photograph, and chip serial number. For the driver's license it stored driving information such as date of expiration, license classification, category of owner, driving violations, and demerit points. Police could use a powerful card reader to access the driving information without access to other protected data, such as health information. As additional applications were added, MyKad would become even more convenient as it eliminated the need to carry numerous cards and facilitated citizens' interactions with government services and commercial transactions.

Cost-Effectiveness

MyKad offered a cost savings to the government by not having to produce numerous cards for various functions, and to the citizens by not having to purchase numerous cards. The government reported the cost of a GMPC with four applications as 20 ringgit (US $5.26) each and the cost of a GMPC with one application (identity card only) as 10 ringgit (US $2.63). The government was subsidizing 13 ringgit (US $3.42) for each GMPC, since the actual production cost was 33 ringgit for the four applications. NRD Director General Datuk Azizan Ayob assessed the cost as quite reasonable in comparison to the expense of regular identity cards. In a press briefing, he stated: "To pay RM20 for a high-tech document is actually very cheap because even the normal IC application costs between RM10 and RM12" (New Straits Time, 2001). The card was cost-effective when considering its durability. It could last five years under normal circumstances. Prerelease durability tests included putting the card in a washing machine, and it was not damaged.

Efficiency

The shorter time framework for electronic processing of MyKad was a third benefit of the card. Applicants sometimes had to wait months to receive their identity cards, but the new cards were processed in two weeks. Some states of Malaysia had reported a backlog of more than 100,000 identity card applications in the past. The NRD now had one of the most diverse and advanced smart card personalization centers in the world and was capable of personalizing 12,000 cards a day.

Paperless Government

A fourth advantage of MyKad was its potential to facilitate Malaysia's goal of a paperless government, quality service delivery from the government to the citizens, and government responsiveness to the needs of the citizens through e-government. Malaysia's e-government policy initiative emphasized internal operation and service delivery by improving information and processes within the government and enhancing convenience, accessibility, and quality of interactions with the citizens and businesses to strengthen the quality and pace of policy development, coordination, and enforcement (MSC, 2001).

Malaysia had promoted the transition to e-government with the launching of the MSC in 1996. Through the MSC, Malaysia was one of the first countries to establish soft infrastructure of cyber-laws to handle legal transactions and processes in e-government. As the premier MSC flagship initiative, MyKad was the access key to enable citizens to benefit from e-government and other e-services of telemedicine, smart schools, borderless marketing centers, worldwide manufacturing webs, and R&D clusters under development in Malaysia.

Future plans were to expand the use of the card to include security access to homes and offices and to pay for public transportation and tolls. Universal proliferation of MyKad with uploaded applications would allow the government to expand services to and interactions with its citizens beyond the MSC and Klang Valley area.

Security

The security features of MyKad offered additional benefits to Malaysia. As a fifth advantage, the government could reduce the amount of fraud occurring with identity cards and birth certificates because of the biometrics technology of the GMPC. MyKad used face and fingerprints as unique physical characteristics to authenticate the identity of the cardholder. Instead of thumbprints, Malaysia's GMPC had two thumbprint minutiae, digitized thumbprints. A thumb scanner was used to match prints, as the cardholder's own thumb was scanned for verification. The GMPC revealed an image of the cardholder's face on the card under ultraviolet light. The card also had a hologram of the hibiscus, Malaysia's national flower, and latent tags that revealed duplication of or tampering with the card. The word "salinan" (copy) would appear if someone attempted to scan or photocopy the card. Also, MyKad's security feature of writer-disablement of nonchangeable, critical data such as name and date of birth after data entry would impede fraudulent changes that occurred with traditional paper and plastic documents.

This same technology offered an additional benefit of security measures against extremist groups or potential violators entering the country illegally or carrying out government-threatening activities. With universal card proliferation, citizens and residents were registered with the government and the card would record their financial transactions, government activities, medical data, and travel information if needed by the authorities. This information would be accessible only to the appropriate enforcement agencies and officials. Moreover, the authorities would not have access to all data on the card because of the firewalls on the card. The agencies would have access restricted to information related to the violation.

The Personal Data Protection law, scheduled for final draft in March 2002, would ideally enhance the privacy rights of citizens by protecting the privacy of personal data and information in computer systems and transmitted over networks, but the government must first protect national and public security interests. As for the Personal Data Protection law protecting privacy rights, Energy, Communications and Multimedia Minister Datuk Amar Leo Moggie stated: "It is important to recognize that individual privacy rights are never absolute" (Raslan, 2001).

Wan Mohamed Ariffin, GMPC project director of the NRD, acknowledged the cutting-edge security measures of MyKad and Malaysia's willingness to cooperate with technology sharing after the September 11, 2001 terrorist attacks on the World Trade Center in New York City and the Pentagon in Washington, DC. "A lot of governments including the U.S. will be looking at better identification systems to monitor the movement of people within countries after last week's terror attack. . . . We are willing to share our technology. It could be part of the solution to the security issue" (Daily News, 2001).

Leadership

As a sixth benefit of MyKad, the development of a public-sector, multipurpose smart card catapulted Malaysia into a global leadership role in information and communication technology (ICT). Although smart cards had long been used in Europe, Malaysia was the first country to introduce a national multipurpose card. Small countries frequently viewed information technology as a means to level the playing field between large and small countries. Small, less-industrialized countries do not need to dismantle the infrastructure of the industrial age as many of the large states do to move forward in information technology (Brown, 1996). Small, industrialized or industrializing countries viewed advanced technology as a way to leapfrog over the steps of industrialization.

Other countries and locations were following suit in developing multipurpose smart cards. Japan planned to issue 1.2 million contactless smart cards in more than 50 municipalities as a test in March 2002, with future plans for multi-application cards and a national roll-out in 2003. The cards were not mandatory for the beta test or national roll-out. Kishimoto Shuhei, head of the smart card pilot project for the Ministry of International Trade and Industry of Japan, stated in an interview, "We're trying to implement the most advanced smart card systems. We want to leap-frog the smart card technology in Europe and the United States" (CardTechnology, 2001). South Korea hosted SmartWorld 2001, the country's first international conference on smart cards. India was scheduled to host the Smart Card @India Conference in March 2002 on the development, implementation, and use of smart cards. A study of smart card markets in Australia, New Zealand, China, Hong Kong, India, Japan South Korea, Malaysia, the Philippines, Singapore, Taiwan, and Thailand, by the international marketing and consulting training company of Frost & Sullivan, revealed an increasing demand for multi-application smart cards from 1998 to 1999. The Latin American smart card market continued to surge, and South Africa had introduced a smart card program (Frost & Sullivan, 2001).

In the United States, the Department of Defense (DOD) started testing 84,000 multipurpose smart cards in October 2000 in preparation for its Common Access (CAC) program, which began in November 2001. DOD planned to issue cards to its 4 million eligible personnel via 900 DOD issuance centers worldwide by the end of 2000 (Department of Defense, 2001). The Java programmable smart card, good for three years, had a data information capacity of 32K and a contract allowing for technology updates to avoid a lag in applying advanced applications. It was used for personal identification, physical building and controlled space access, and network and systems access. Personal information on the card included the cardholder's name, personal identification number, picture, and fingerprint. To secure data and access, the card possessed personal key information functions of authentication, encryption, decryption, and digital signing. Other applications included deployment readiness, personnel tracking, property accountability, and food service. Future applications would include biometrics and medical information.

Signs pointed to Malaysia's global leadership role in smart card development. It received the World Quality International Award (Gold Category) in Paris in 2001 for the GMPC. Also, Malaysia hosted the Cardex Asia 2001 Conference, the first international smart card meeting held in Malaysia in September 2001. Another indication of Malaysia's global acknowledgment for smart card development was MyKad's nomination for Best Technological Innovation category in 2001 for the annual SESAMES award and its selection as one of the three finalists. The SESAMES award is affiliated with CARTES, the world's largest conference and exhibition on the latest innovations and issues in smart card technology held annually in Paris (CARTES, 2001).

Global attention to Malaysia's multipurpose smart card and its security measures heightened as private and public sectors in the United States raised the issue of biometrics technology and airport security following the terrorist attacks of September 11, 2001. Richard Norton, executive director of the International Biometric Industry Association, stated that since the September 11 attacks, "people see a compelling case for it [deploying biometric systems at airports]." These systems would identify people by such characteristics as fingerprints, facial structure, or iris patterns (Langlois, 2001).

To enhance its global recognition, a Malaysian delegation attended the World Congress on Information Technology (WCIT) in Adelaide, Australia, from February 26 to March 1, 2002. The meeting hosted about 1,800 top-level delegates from ICT, business, academia, and government, and was an opportunity to network with ICT industry leaders and policymakers. Malaysia planned to make a bid to host the next WCIT in 2008.

❖ CHALLENGES OF MYKAD

Although the universal proliferation of MyKad offered explicit advantages for Malaysia, it was not without challenges. Opponents to the universal roll-out of the project addressed a number of concerns.

Acceptance

One of the main issues was the validity and acceptance of MyKad. Some of the private- and public-sector agencies had not accepted the card because they questioned the legality of the document. Two months after its initial use in September 2001, some enforcement agency personnel still did not recognize the card and refused to accept it. NRD Director General Datuk Azizan Ayob said, "Misunderstandings arose in cases where agencies have refused to accept it during transactions" (Saithuruka, 2001). In one case, a RTD officer summoned a driver charging that MyKad had not been gazetted. Azizan declared that MyKad had already been gazetted on August 1, 2001. He reassured the public on November 2, 2001, in a press conference statement: "Those who have the cards should not hesitate to use them and the agencies involved must accept the new identification card" (Saithuruka, 2001).

The NRD reported in many cases the public perceived MyKad as only a new identity card and was not aware of its applications. Many Malaysians, although familiar with carrying an identification card, were not used to the concept of one card with a host of information on it. Wan Mohamed Ariffin acknowledged the need for more education to increase awareness about the card. NRD planned a massive promotion program for the card in December 2001. Azizan noted that, meanwhile, cardholders would be allowed to carry the old identity card and old driving license *and* the new MyKad.

Some of the questions about the card's validity stemmed from a lack of fingerprints on the card. Azizan reported that Tabung Haji branches and banks had refused to accept the card because no thumbprints were visible on the card. The thumbprint minutiae, however, were embedded in the microchip, requiring special card readers to differentiate the prints. The private sector would have to purchase the devices to access the data on the card. The RTD officer needed to use one of the 800 key ring readers made available to the agency to read the driver's license information.

Security

Even after the cards were accepted as valid, security concerns about MyKad remained as a second challenge. Questions surrounded who got access to data and could alter records. Were the data encryption standards sufficient? How would network security threats affect the data on MyKad? Although firewall, encryption, and write-protected standards existed, MyKad was not security risk-proof. Smart cards in general were not hack-proof. Hackers had challenged the smart card system of DirecTV and gained access to free TV programming (Star, 2001).

Kevin Poulsen, editorial director of Security Focus, a security technology firm, warned that using smart cards to prevent violation of immigration laws could make smart cards a hacking goal for counterfeiters, who were currently making fake identification documents for unregistered migrants (Star, 2001). In Malaysia, village leaders had already been charged with helping foreigners obtain identity cards during the one-week registration exercise. Allegedly, the foreigners paid the village heads to sign their identity card applications. The NRD in the village of Banggi uncovered the identity fraud. The paper fraud could become a counterfeiter's priority to alter passport data or to create bogus identity in registration exercises to obtain the GMPC identification cards (New Sabah Times, 2001).

According to a survey of members of commercial organizations in Malaysia in 2001, the top three security threats were viruses; unauthorized use of IS systems, e-mail, or applications; and denial of service attacks that flood a Web site or telecommunications resource making it inaccessible. Any of the three cyberattacks could make information inaccessible via the card with Internet connections. Malaysia had already witnessed the hacking of its parliament's Web site in 2000. The Kedah government's Web site had also been hacked. Opposition Democratic Action Party Chairman Lim Kit Siang argued the lack of security measures to control hacking raised a larger issue related to MyKad—the futility of the MSC e-government flagship (Lim, 2001).

The Government Online Study, conducted by the Social and Government Division of Taylor Nelson Sofres in 2001, reported that Malaysia lagged behind most countries in e-government usage. The main reason cited was security. Only 11% of Malaysians reported using the Internet to access government information, transact with government services online, or provide data to government agencies. More than half of the Malaysians polled stated that they worried about providing the government with personal or credit card information via the Internet (Sofres, 2001). Lim questioned why e-government was not more widely used in Malaysia if the MSC was Malaysia's world display of cutting-edge information technology and e-government was one of its flagships. As Lim stated on his party's homepage:

> If the MSC is Malaysia's "gift to the world" and electronic government one of the seven MSC flagship applications, then there is no reason why in an international survey on e-government adoption, Malaysia lagged behind many of the 27 countries surveyed in the study based on global and national benchmarks relating to the use of government services online and perceptions of safety when providing personal information to Government. (Lim, 2001)

Would MyKad, a key access to e-government, possess the security measures to garner increased use of e-government?

Use of PKI to secure corporate infrastructure had reportedly increased in Malaysia. The digital certificates used strong encryption for both the server and client end. Since it started in September 2000, the MSC Trustgate encryption program had sold more than 10,000 server certificates (for data confidentiality and Web site authentication) and client certificates (for data integrity and identity authentication) in Malaysia and other parts of Asia (Lee, 2001). However, the National ICT Security and Emergency Response Centre (NISER) conducted a study of 205 organizations in Malaysia in April 2001, and found a low level of PKI adoption. The use of PKI was 8% in the public/finance sector and 5% in the private sector (Niser, 2001).

Privacy Rights

The security issue was also related to a third challenge of MyKad, the potential violation of privacy rights with data obtained from an individual's card. Federation of Malaysian Consumers Association (FOMCA) President Datuk Hamdan Adnan questioned if the issues of security and privacy overshadowed the advancement in technology:

> On the upside, it [MyKad] is indeed a giant step in technology and would make things easier. But as a consumer, I am worried about privacy intrusion and more important, the security of the card. Will the government give guarantees if anything happens, and what would be the recourse? (Kam, 2001)

Wan Mohamed Ariffin, project director of MyKad, admitted that in addition to the public worry about the security of MyKad, the government's possession of citizens' information was an issue. He maintained, however, that MyKad would not restrict their freedom. He stated: "The other fear is that Big Brother (the government) will constantly keep tabs on you. But consider this: military people have always carried a special ID and in no way has it impeded their freedom" (Kam, 2001). Taiwan's national smart card plan evoked the same public criticism (Liu, 1999).

Although parliamentary debate had addressed the Personal Data Protection legislation scheduled for March 2002, and its intention to protect the privacy of personal information and data, in December 2001 there was still no legislation to protect rights of privacy. Minister Datuk Seri Dr. Rais Yatim of the Prime Minister's Office, in commenting on cyber-law training for the judiciary and police, acknowledged the need to have data protection laws: "Malaysia law still lags behind in the need to protect the individual from trauma arising from personal data loss. I believe there is now a need to protect the individual from the unscrupulous acts of others" (Wani Muthiah, 2001). Another concern

Rais identified was the lack of privacy laws as an impediment to international trade and commercial activities. The European Union Data Protection Directive required member nations to guarantee that their laws protected information related to European citizens when transmitted beyond Europe.

Coordination of Implementation

Coordinating the government agencies, a fourth challenge to the implementation of MyKad, had been no easy task. Before the official launch of MyKad on September 5, 2001, Home Ministry Secretary-General Aseh, Chairman of the GMPC Taskforce, met with agency representatives to coordinate a smooth, seamless implementation of the card. As Aseh noted: "In our meetings almost all the problems and inconveniences were resolved and these departments agreed to the smooth implementation of the smart cards for the use of the public" (Krishnamoorthy, 2001). The main obstacles to implementation had been lack of sufficient card readers at various locations and misunderstanding about the thumbprint authentication. NRD underestimated the number of card readers necessary for enforcement officers. It distributed only 800 KRRs for reading driver's license data. NRD also supplied "a few units" of the Morphotouch 200 and desktop readers, which could be installed on PCs and could read thumbprint and card data. NRD planned to purchase additional card readers for public agencies, but private-sector units had to purchase their own devices to access information from a government card.

Cost

Although the low cost per card was a benefit, the overall cost of the MyKad program was a fifth disadvantage. By 2001, Malaysia was in an economic downturn, with low trade anticipated after the economic recession in the United States and slow growth after the September 11 terrorist attacks. NRD received about RM267 million to implement the GMPC project in the Klang Valley, which included the cost of setting up the 12 GSCs for all MyKad-related transactions, deploying CADs and readers, and developing infrastructure to support MyKad. The cost was an incomplete estimate because of additional readers NRD purchased to send to public agencies.

Scalability

A sixth challenge of Malaysia's MyKad was its scalability and accessibility for universal proliferation in the country. Starting in April 2001, the GMPC was available to the public in the MSC, the ICT-focus area of Malaysia, and the affluent Klang Valley region. Card availability to the public in Sabah and Sarawak was scheduled for January 2002. National roll-out of the GMPC was targeted to begin in 2003 with an estimated five to eight years to complete the entire process. As of December 2001, the GMPC was only available in the affluent Klang Valley area. Would the government be able to offer universal cards by 2011? In remote areas of Sabah, some of the Bumiputeras did not have birth certificates and registration identification cards, the supporting documents necessary to apply for MyKad. MP Datuk Yong Teck Lee had raised the issue of the lack of records during parliamentary question time on May 3, 2001.

The Ministry of Home Affairs replied that through the NRD, it was in the process of collecting data on the number of people without records, and efforts were still under way to issue birth certificates and identity cards to them via a mobile exercise involving appropriate authorities. The NRD would need to identify all citizens and residents without supporting documents and issue these records before issuing smart cards. The prime minister's MyKad Taskforce could recommend a special nationwide campaign to get registered to encourage support. University students of the Bumiputeras group, sharing a similar language, could earn credit by going to remote areas to expedite data collection.

Also, the NRD had to ensure that the people receiving birth certificates and identity cards were qualified to do so. Once people possessed these two documents—the support credentials—to obtain a GMPC, they would legitimately be part of the system.

Instability

Increasing Internet use in Malaysia offered a seventh indirect disadvantage to the proliferation of MyKad. IDC Malaysia reported that 2.07 million people had Internet access in Malaysia at the end of 2000, with an increase of 20% expected by 2005. Plans for MyKad included applications that would increase cardholders' use of the Internet. An increase in Internet use could offer additional challenges to the government in controlling the media. More people and media agents would have access to the Internet without government control and, thus, more potential avenues for criticizing the government.

In February 2001, the government barred independent journalists, including those from the online newspaper *Malaysiakini*, from attending government press conferences or interviewing department and agency heads. Speaking to the parliament in April 2001, Prime Minister Mahathir criticized "total press freedom" and announced the government's plans to revise existing media laws. In support of the prime minister's statements, Minister of Energy, Communications and Multimedia Moggie stated the nation's outdated cyber-laws were in need of replacement. Critics questioned if the ban on independent journalists, along with the call for revision of media laws, was the start of Internet censorship, a move that Prime Minister Mahathir vowed to never make because it was a threat to the development of technology and the MSC. One part of the MSC Bill of Guarantees was that there would be no censorship of the Internet. As a multiracial society of Malays, Chinese, and Indians, there was a history of volatile race riots in 1969, a resulting state of emergency, and more recent riots in Malaysia and neighboring multiracial Indonesia. The government feared disgruntled populations or extremist groups would rally support to challenge the political system, especially via the Internet.

❖ WHAT TO DO?

Smart card technology was evolving at a rapid pace and would require advanced research and training to keep MyKad updated with ISO standards and appropriate applications for Malaysia and e-services. Malaysia might have to rely on outsourcing to foreign IT contractors and companies for vital technology skills. Was the government moving too fast to launch a universal roll-out of MyKad without the properly trained human resource support? A national survey could have revealed widespread support for FOMCA president Hamdan Adnan's sentiment:

> There doesn't seem to be any other country doing this [MyKad] at present which means we're the first. It would appear hard to justify implementing a smart card system in a developing country like ours. It makes more sense to wait and learn from other countries

that are technologically more advanced and learn from their mistakes. (Kam, 2001)

The card as a benefit could simultaneously be a disadvantage if the country could not maintain the technology. ICT training and emphasis were crucial for technology to move forward. Schools, government, and community training programs were available but might not be adequate for preparing a national core of skilled programmers and IT specialists to update the smart card technology and expand its applications.

Malaysia had benefited from nongovernment organizations (NGO) and programs to improve ICT training and expansion. In one such example, Lin Mui Kiang, a former government bureaucrat and a member of the NGO WorldView International, established a project called SMASY, which stood for Smart Masyarakat ("Smart Community"), to expand information technology to the rural areas with a government grant of $187,000. The village, Kampung Raja Musa, was the beta site for her project because the village leaders were receptive to the plan and the village had the necessary infrastructure of accessible roads and reliable phone and electrical lines. Kampung Raja Musa, 120 kilometers south of Kuala Lumpur, was a predominately Malay-Muslim village of 1,150 residents. The project included a Chinese community and an Indian community. Databases were accessible via kiosk or computer, with helpful information on dealing with government bureaucracies (Arjuna, 2001).

Democratic Action Party National Vice-Chairman and MP Dr. Tan Seng Giaw argued that grants targeting rural areas for IT training were not enough to overcome Malaysia's digital divide. Areas outside *and within* the cities needed IT training to develop. Tan Seng Giaw recommended a National Digital Policy in 2000, separate from Malaysia's New Economic Policy.

The government proposed a study to examine the effect of ICT on society and gain a better understanding of the ICT development direction for Malaysia. A program, Subang Jaya, was earmarked as a test for migration to the e-world in a project known as SJ2005 Smart Community Program. The project was to evaluate and study the social, educational, political, economic, and technological impact of ICT on communities. It was a lived-in community case study to test access to ICT and its transformation of the world in which we lived and worked.

In the 2001 budget, Minister of Finance Tun Daim Zainuddin emphasized the importance of continuing ICT training. ICT-based applications were crucial for enhancing the country's productivity and competitiveness. To narrow the digital divide, the budget would provide tax incentives to individuals and companies that invested in IT equipment and industry. Government employees could apply for a computer loan once every five years. Daim called for teachers and lecturers to return to their home villages to share their expertise and experience with the rural population.

Opposition party leader Lim, frustrated with massive pilot projects, recommended the appointment of an e-minister to handle the responsibility of the government's IT agenda. MyKad was part of that agenda. How would the MyKad Evaluation Team decide the fate of MyKad?

❖ REFERENCES

Arjuna, R. (2001). Lin Mui Kiang: Defender of the rural poor. *AsiaWeek,* June 29. Retrieved February 6, 2002, from www.asiaweek.com/ asiaweek/technology/article/0,8707,132169,00.html

Atkinson, R. D. (2001). How technology can help make air travel safe again. Progressive Policy Institute Policy Report, September 2001. Retrieved February 6, 2002, from www.ppionline.org/documents/Airport_Security_092501.pdf

Bowen, C. (2001). Suddenly, it's all about security. *Card Technology,* November.

Brown, C. L. (1996, May). International collaborative education and research using information and communication technology: Multi-level strategies for the twenty-first century. Paper presented at the International Conference on Higher Education in the Twenty-first Century: Mission and Challenge in Developing Countries. Hanoi, Vietnam.

CARTES. (2001). The SESAMES 2001 nominees are . . . Retrieved February 6, 2002, from www.cartes.com/en/contenu/sesames/nominee.htm

Caterinicchia, D. (2001). DOD preps smart card roll out. *Federal Computer Week,* November 5. Retrieved February 6, 2002, from www.fcw.com/fcw/articles/2001/1105/tec-dod-11-05-01.asp

Department of Defense, U.S. (2001, May). *Department of Defense common access card (CAC).* Presented at Smart Card Project Manager's Meeting. Retrieved February 6, 2002, from egov.gov/smartgov/information/mdixon_051001xcpmg/sld001.htm

Exploring smart card options. (2001). *The Star,* October 30. Retrieved February 6, 2002, from www.yasmin.com.my/News/Archive/exploring_smartcard/exploring_smartcard.htm

Frost & Sullivan. (2000). Pan Asia smart card markets. Report No. 4180-11. Frost & Sullivan: San Antonio, TX. Retrieved February 6, 2002, from www.frost.com.

Japan to launch test of voluntary national ID card. (2001). *CardTechnology*, December. Retrieved February 6, 2002, from www.ct-ctst.com/Archives/

Kam, P. (2001). A card for all reasons. *The Star*, December 13. Retrieved February 6, 2002, from www.yasmin.com.my/News/Archive/card_reason/card_for_all_reason.htm

Krishnamoorthy, M. (2001). Aseh: Gov't. agencies must accept MyKad. *The Star*, November 5. Retrieved February 6, 2002, from www.yasmin.com.my/News/Archive/govt_agencies/govt_agencies.htm

Langlois, G. (2001). Facing the need for biometrics. *Federal Computer Week*, October. Retrieved February 6, 2002, from www.fcw.com/fcw/articles/2001/1001/news-bio-10-01-01.asp

Lee Min Keong. (2001, June). PKI awareness growing in Malaysia. Retrieved February 6, 2002, from www.asiafeatures.com/current_affairs/0106,1505,01.html

Lim Kit Sang. (2001). Media statement December 17. Retrieved February 6, 2002, from www.malaysia.net/dap/lks1349.htm

Liu Ching-Yi. (1999, June). How smart is the IC card? The proposed national smart card plan, Boo strategy, electronic commerce, and the emerging danger to online privacy in Asia. Paper presented at 9th Annual Conference of the Internet Society, INET'99. San Jose, California. Retrieved February 6, 2002, from www.isoc.org/inet99/posters/439/

Mahathir, M. (1991, February). The way forward—Vision 2020. Paper presented at the Malaysian Business Council. Kuala Lumpur. Retrieved February 6, 2002, from www.jaring.my/isis/mbc/2020.htm

Mahathir, M. (1995, September). Speech by the prime minister at the dinner in conjunction with the launching of the Academy of Sciences Malaysia. Kuala Lumpur.

Matthews, J. (2001). Government issues smartcards to citizens. *Nikkei Electronics Asia*, June. Retrieved February 6, 2002, from www.nikkeibp.asiabiztech.com/nea/200106/comy_132303.html

MSC. (2001). E-government cluster. Retrieved February 6, 2002, from www.msc-expo.com.my/eg/background.html

Multifunction smart card chips coming up. (2001). *Global Sources Security & Safety*, September 17. Retrieved February 6, 2002, from www.globalsources.com/MAGAZINE/SECURITY/0111/N091701.HTM

Multipurpose smart card available now. (2001). *New Straits Time*, April 13. Retrieved February 6, 2002, from www.yasmin.com.my/News/Archive/Multipurpose_Smart_Card/multipurpose_smart_card.htm

NISER. (2001). NISER ICT security survey for Malaysia 2000/2001, November 7. Retrieved February 6, 2002, from www.niser.org.my/cgi-bin/survey/survey.cgi?ac=exec

Raslan S. (2001). Data protection law to balance private, public interests. *The Star*, November 29. Retrieved February 6, 2002, from www.niser.org.my/news/2001_11_29_04.html

"Smart" identity cards could be new weapon in war on terrorism. (2001). *Daily News-Online Edition*, September 22. Retrieved February 6, 2002, from origin.dailynews.lk/2001/09/22/wor02.html

Sofres, T. N. (2001). Security concerns limit growth of e-government—Survey findings. Retrieved February 6, 2002, from www.tnsofres.com/press/pressstory.cfm?storyID=544

Streejit P. (2001). Gov't. says public smart cards safe. *CNET.com*, May 28. Retrieved February 6, 2002, from asia.cnet.com/newstech/communications/0,39001141,13032951,00.htm

Village Heads Arrested. (2001). *New Sabah Times*, June 23. Retrieved February 6, 2002, from www.newsabahtimes.com.my/June/22.6/local1.htm

Wani Muthiah. (2001). Need for Cyber Law Training. *The Star*, November 30. Retrieved February 6, 2002, from www.niser.org.my/news/2001_11_30_02.html

Smart Card Overview and Tutorials

Cagliostro, C. Primer on smart cards. Retrieved February 6, 2002, from www.scia.org/knowledgebase/aboutSmartCards/primer.htm

Cards now! Asia. Retrieved February 6, 2002, from www.cardsnowasia.com/

CARTES. (2001). Glossary. (Smart card technology.) Retrieved February 6, 2002, from www.cartes.com/en/frames/news.htm

Everett, David B. (2001). Smart card technology: Introduction to smart cards. Retrieved February 6, 2002, from www.smartcard.co.uk/articles/intro2sc.html

Smart card library. (Features more than 555 smart cards.) Retrieved February 6, 2002, from www.smartcard.co.uk/library.html

Smart card links. Retrieved February 6, 2002, from www.mcard.umich.edu/otherLinks.htm

Smart card news. Retrieved February 6, 2002, from www.smartcard.co.uk/

Smart card resource center. AMERKORE international. Retrieved February 6, 2002, from www.smart-card.com/biometric.htm

Smart card tutorial: An online multimedia presentation. United States General Services Administration (GSA). Retrieved February 6, 2002, from egov.gov/smartgov/tutorial/smartcard_foyer.htm

Index

About the Editor

Terrel L. Rhodes is Professor of Public Administration and Vice Provost for Curriculum and Undergraduate Studies at Portland State University. He has experience nationally and internationally in local government training. His most recent book is *Republicans in the South: Voting for the White House, Voting for the Statehouse.*

About the Contributors

Patricia Maloney Alt is Professor, Department of Health Sciences, and Coordinator, Clinician-Administrator Transition Program, at Towson University. She was previously Aging Policy Coordinator for the Maryland State Department of Health and Mental Hygiene (DHMH) and has been a consultant to federal, state, and local agencies. She is the Chair of the Towson University Institutional Review Board for the Protection of Human Research Participants (IRB) and also serves on the DHMH IRB.

Cheryl L. Brown is Associate Professor of Political Science at the University of North Carolina at Charlotte. She is a specialist in Chinese politics, international relations, and e-government.

Maureen Brown is Associate Professor in the public administration program at the University of North Carolina at Charlotte. She is a national consultant on information technology systems and was the principal investigator on the U.S. Department of Justice COPS-MORE grant received by the City of Charlotte Metropolitan Police Department.

Robert J. Gassner is Vision Council Manager with the United Way of the Columbia-Willamette. He holds a master of public administration (MPA) from Portland State University and was formerly executive director of Healthy Communities, Inc.

Sherril B. Gelmon is Associate Professor of Public Health in the Department of Public Administration at Portland State University. She is a nationally recognized consultant on assessment and serves as a judge for the national Malcolm Baldridge Award program.

Carole L. Jurkiewicz is Milton J. Womack Professor for Developing Scholars, Public Administration Institute in the E. J. Ourso College of

Business Administration at Louisiana State University, and Chair of the Ethics Section of the American Society for Public Administration.

Gary R. Rassel is Associate Professor of Political Science and Coordinator of the master of public administration program at the University of North Carolina at Charlotte. He is coauthor, with Elizabethann O'Sullivan, of the textbook *Research Methods for Public Administrators*.

Linda E. Swayne is Professor of Marketing in the William and Ida Friday College of Business Administration at the University of North Carolina at Charlotte, where she serves as chair of the department. She is the author of numerous books in marketing and health administration.

David F. Thompson is Chief Operating Officer and managing principal of Freeman White, Inc., of Charlotte, NC. He has a master of public administration (MPA) from North Carolina State University. He also served as a county manager of three counties over a 15-year period.